**NDUE UK**

# ITHACA OF THE WORD

Poetry

Translated
by
**PETER TASE**

WWW.LULU.COM
UNITED STATES OF AMERICA

# NDUE UKAJ - ITHACA OF THE WORD

The opinions expressed in this manuscript are solely the opinions of the author and do not represent the opinions or thoughts of the publisher. The author represents and warrants that s/he either owns or has the legal right to publish all material in this book.

### "ITHACA OF THE WORD"
All Rights Reserved.
Copyright © 2010  Ndue Ukaj

*Translated & Edited*: Peter Tase

*Introduction*: Petrit Palushi
*Afterword:* Anton Gojçaj

*Cover and Interior Design*: Piro Tase

This book may not be reproduced, transmitted, or stored in whole or in part by any means, including graphic, electronic, or mechanical without the express written consent of the publisher except in the case of brief quotations embodied in critical articles and reviews.

ISBN: 978-1-4461-2538-0

**PRINTED IN THE UNITED STATES OF AMERICA**
WWW.LULU.COM
http//www.lulu.com

To:

*My beloved family,
Edita,
Luis and Izabela*

# NDUE UKAJ - ITHACA OF THE WORD

## PREFACE

"Ithaca of the Word" is the symbol of modern Albanian poetry, literature and patriotism expressed through the majestic means of communication and these are words and verses incorporated in every poem written by Ndue Ukaj in this edition presently published in English language.

It has always been said that translation from one language to another reduces the level of meaning, emotions, passion and structure, indeed in this book the opposite has occured: Comparing the poems side by side in the two languages one will find that the level of emphasis, emotional presence and the unique patriotic style of Ndue Ukaj have not vanished. Therefore should be emphasized once again that content and style remain as vivid and splendid as they were in the original version in Albanian language.

It has been an honor and great privilege to have this opportunity and work together with Ndue Ukaj in the field of Albanian Literature and Poetry.

This volume shows once more the unique style and patriotic ideals of the author.

The one hundred poems in this volume undoubtedly place Ndue Ukaj in the Modern Albanian Authors' Hall of Fame.

He embodies new writing technique and many skills that ought to be admired by all his colleagues.

Ukaj is a symbol of freedom expressed through words and verses.

PETER TASE

*September 20th, 2010*

## FOREWORD

*Distinguished Aspects in Subject and Style
on the First Volume of Poetry
by*
**NDUE UKAJ**

"Ithaca of the Word" is the first book of poetry written by Ndue Ukaj. This is the fruit of a long career and of many years dedicated to the study of Litterature, Literary criticisism and Creative writting. The poetry of Ndue Ukaj is a masterpiece that attempts to come down at the soul of every individual, in that misterious labyrinth; were at once transcends to us by knowing more about this distinguished Albanian Author. Ukaj's poetry represents a turbulent spirit and a dedicated writer engulfed under the turbulence of creation that make his poetry not only a lyrical poetry but also epical and dramatical. Every verse touches upon the concerns for our world today and this unique content vitalises Ukaj's poetry as a whole.

This happens as it has been said rightfully in the past by Simborska: "That Poets will always be assigned to projects that only they can accomplish successfully."

The poetry of the "Ithaca of the word" is not only focused under a certain vicious circle that contains only one topic, but naturally the topics are more broad and take other styles of variations and the view of the reader will not be focused only on one topical view. Indeed the opposite is true, the vision of the reader penetrates through every square inch of the human body and it includes patriotism, romanticizm, mortality and above all it causes saddness in the human spirit. In this context, it is impossible to bring poetry even closer to human spirit, to enrich it even more with the vital substance of life and to make it more flexible. This requirements are all met by the author which has identified himself as a well versed and very talented. It is natural that the reader will enjoy this work of poetry and will read it many times and everytime will experience a variation of feelings while expressing his or her desire to keep alive the images developed from reading this work of poetry. Inside these distinguished variations in theme and style, are unraveled naturally many small topics, well versed ideas and other subjects enlivened thanks to Ukaj's creativity in poetry and his wisdom in the use of simple and profound words that from time to time cause pathos.

From the first impression it is visible that "Ithaca of the Word" has the concept of present time and the past, these are the two principal mile stones in the one hundred titles of this presentation. The concept of time is more of a guide of the language and thematic focus that anything else. Images shift from one era to the next, righteously are intertwined with other images, the redundant characters disapear suddenly, nonfunctionality is also eradicated over the development of every poetry. In the substance remains poetry itself with the subjects that are only related with the avenues of the spirit and soul. In this fashion there is developed the myth of the past and elements of the present time.

Even in the verses dedicated to Father Peter Bogdani, Gergj Fishta, Mother Teresa, Anton Pashku and Ancient Dardania, etc., the presence of myth is aparent and takes an image of contemporaneity as mandatory reflexes in regards to the distant and near past.

I am confident that in the poetry of Ndue Ukaj there are incentives to brake the standard formulas towards the employment of metaphors, which means that the author, in this aspect, is prepared to see the metaphor not only as a simple poetic illustration, but also as a crucial means that energizes the poetical view as a whole with its lack and appearance from time to time. In a few words the whole poetry in this masterpiece can be seen as a poetry that functions only inside a hut full of metaphors.

## *NDUE UKAJ - ITHACA OF THE WORD*

It should be noted that in the " Ithaca of the Word", there is an initiative to implement a long poetry, and this transformational form, energizes and brings more value to poetry, it distinguishes poetry as a literary work of full images, increases the understanding and density of the thought, and makes possible the full poetical expression of the author. Taking into consideration all these incredible values encompassed in this first volume of poetry by Ndue Ukaj; this work is welcomed with its own code of conduct, looking upon its own nitch including unique communication technique and taking the lead as a poetry with a particular expression, were a group of metaphors enlighten even the darkest points of the content introduced and presented to the reader.

PETRIT PALUSHI

## Godo is not coming

It is raining, the road from Irland is unpassable
The sea cannot be passed with small steps, on rainy nights
When solitude is overwhelming you enjoy the earthquake cracks of the Earth
When pain has no time even for scientific explanation.

Godo is not coming, it is late, infected by the welcoming
Sleeping comfortably, amongst both of our dreams.
He is not coming, neither under the tree of life nor in the theater of wonders,
Under the sleep of expectation which your time doesn't understand...our time.

You are waiting, like the bride on the abandoned bed,
Dreaming of him with open arms as he brings a sack full of dreams
Extending your hands with softness, as in the beloved hair...relaxes there
And prays to your dreams, intertwined through your tall fingers.
Suddenly a bite freezes your body, your hand flies from the sack.
Wiping your forehead you understand that Godo didn't come, neither his enigmatic look.
Nontheless you are not convinced that your dream entered in a sack.
It was tied foreverer just like Godo's arrival.

Surprisingly passed on the other side of the furious river of words
As you pass amongst the dreams full of wonders towards the guards of time
That makes the noise of life in the dream of expectation.
Nearby the time guards

Foster the hope that Godo nevertheless will come.

Godo is not coming, no...!
You are crying, crying frantically until your tears have made a creek
Between your cheeks and your continuous flow of tears.
Where the heart beats are felt like the steps of the unknown
In the gloomy night when grief is around the corner
And even Godo could experience it on his hands and be thrown desperately.

## The Emigrant

The men of my time, Shriveled
As a shell thrown into a dark mud,
Runs in search of time,
Which nobody recognizes, including him.

Lost, with the myth of return burning on his head,
Travels all over the World,
Is not Odyssey, Ithaca is not looking for him
He knows that Penelope is layed in bed and beloved like never before.

Every twilight, when quietness bites.
Unafraid with his head full of passions.
And with the fists full of memories that boil like water on fire
He runs over the meridians of the planet
Without maps and borders, without names nor time
Like a messenger bird, the emigrant
Journeyed through time, reads and re-reads.
Lies to himself endlessly
While numbering centuries on his fingers.
The letter passes the red see on foot.
There is no Nazareth anymore,
Neither the promised land. Saddened!
There is a castle full of death waging myths.
Disappointed.
Very unfortunate, returns running over the frozen sea.
Counts again the years of his life.
On his dreams there are no angels to be invited.
He is extremely delayed.
The return on the fatherland of passions is even far away
Than the remembrance for the departure day towards the endless migration!

The twilight is gone, and time is gone.
He runs ahead pursuing the star of return.
Which vanished together with the star swallowed by the dark clouds.
And the discovery of a dream that smells bad
Somewhere that I don't know where?
The migrant, a contemporary raven,
Lamenting without a break in search of himself.

As Autumn is shaken in front of the winter sleep

## Hemingwayan Waves of Time

The sea is under storms
And the old man fishing without rest
With the ship of the endless times
Searches the shores to his best
A black cloud escorts, with exuberant steps
Life's fish on the reckless sea.
Is an agitated sea and has many wonders
Also has an old man fishing tirelessly,
And a girl fallen in love
Wishing to have the golden fish undoubtedly.
The relentless sea
Is never a peaceful sea,
An attacked ship
Fights for her life
From many storms.
In a misterious depth of the sea under storm
A hungry shark threatens at every cost.
And a broken ship breaks forward with all including the helm.
Icy winter makes the frozen sea like a stone
And the storm grows continuously.

The old man doesn't look at his time,
Screams anxiously and counts the years on his fingers
Is a gloomy night the sea isn't peaceful
Napping from fishing stops and thinks
Now he understands, is the end of life
Was not born to be a people's fisherman
Neither a construction rock.
But his love for life turned it into sailing.
It is sad in these cold icy days
Sea shores are away, there is no wave to rescue him.
The ship of time is challenged while sailing.
She is shaken like the wind with the tired old man.

Until the Sun falls over the sea
And the very hungry girl catches the fish.
The acquarium of memories is on her shadow
As pieces of her compassionate heart.
A big tent of mercifulness.

My God, my Sunday dialogue is even more lonesome
Than the Autumn night with strong winds,
Than the Cathedral sound that disrupts the dark solitude
Crawls it over like a victim of roman times
And the colors of the painter relaxing on the lap of the exotic lady
Waking the next morning with my vision lost which resembles
To my dialogue with poetry on Sunday...!

## Fatal Horse

When I was here
In front of me was my time,
In that world when I wasn't there
In the Trojan war
Inside the dreamless trojan horse.
Were I dismantled the fatal dreams
Of the loss of Ithaca.

I saw Helena treespassing over the wall
Saw her...covered with a transparent cloth
behind which her fatal beauty
was shining like stars for Achilles
And endless writters that scream
With their majestic verses time after time.
The writter's day never ends
In the magic twentyfour hours
while designing all kinds of wonders
Including the road to return in the country of passions

I saw Helena in the sweetest moments
Behind which was hiding with anxiety
A lustfull body of love
And a mountain of enigmas never unveiled.

This is why I never withdrew my desire
To walk together with the wind of ice ages
And become acquainted with the rivers of lies
Which dissolved our spirit and the fatal river
In our nameless roads. Without Helena!
With numbness from our escape off legends
And the design of fatal horses day and night
That are grunting continuously over our tempted heads.

## NDUE UKAJ - ITHACA OF THE WORD

Enclosed inside the concrete ego
Focus my vision towards emptyness
While eating dried figs
And drinking a glass of wine older than poetry itself

While I glance over Ithaca
And see how the shadow of fatal horse
Navigates as an amateur in the art of life
Towards the burned bedroom of Helena.

## Melancholy

Affliction is falling and washes his tired hands
In the briny water closer to the castle of thoughts
Where the fondness of birds is sniffed quietly
Hungry to sing freely in a clear sky

Affliction falls and washes his tired hands
Over the sweet bulbs spoiled by the useless sleep
In the middle of the day when midnight dreams are shaken
And the bird's escape from lightning that hurts his eyes.

Affliction falls in the tired hands, were it sketches liberty
Hides on his sweaty shirt the torn letter
Where undecifered drawing is found. Doesn't understand
The bird has no nest to return to freedom, Walks on the sky paths.

Affliction falls and quikly cleans its tired hands
Nearby the resque ship her feet are engulfed in the sand
The bird has no fatherland, neither a nest of happyness
His fatherland is time and the mercy of storms.

## Ruins of Love

A Sun beam goes straight to your wonderful eyes,
It is lightning there were vision is twisted, my love
Your softness and past times resound with the passion of remembrance as in acquarium
The sun beam sweetly passes through and touches all your body.
Fondle softly your nudified arms, my beautiful one.
Later you shake your soft vision towards the beautiful beam, then said:
Love is endlessly beautiful only when there is love.
And take great walk like in the garden of Eden, near the river of silence.
With passion over your shoulder, full of inflamed desires, full of wonders.
Dreamed through the times gathered in our fist deeper and deeper.
Over the ruins of Love you walk like a dancer or butterfly that touches the sky.
And your sweet, very sweet smile lays in the galaxy.
Without wonders for the burning times with harsh looks.
I seize love on my hand like a gift for you, for your beauty.
And the sun beams that warm your icy bones in the painful sleep.
Your kiss is extremely sweet, endlessly sweet.
Night is wearing black clothes, you are shining like a star, my dear love.
Then reacts quietly on her disturbed spirit.
Undressing the locked thoughts through the noise of intoxicating time.
Soft sounds from the spirit's music making a shade.
You are quiet, noise is quite... while your interiors
Turn into butterflies throughout the emptied room of thoughts.
Nothing, nothing, my love

Is more valuable than your layed body sniffing the aroma of love.
My thirsty eye on the obscured angels is lost,
deppressed...Oh.
Completely lost my mind to enter deeply on you my love.

## Illusion of Time

My toung moves unfrightened
In the shiverings' waterfalls of the past
A frozen tear like an Antarctic ice over me
Does a frightening shade to the deformed roof.

Night falls quietly like a beloved woman layed down
Where illusions of eternity are frighteningly fed
Where future illusions frighteningly knock
Where daunting fire, lightning times erupt
The melted times on the lost calendars
When groaning went throughout the sky
Earth swallows us with rotten spiders in obscuring darkness
Tied in our legs worst and even worst.
While a lonely bird flies in the endless sky.
Abandoned his nest destroyed from the storm
In the sky sketches a red box
It is not Pandoras box, has no sins.
And it doesn't foster the illusions of eternity
Only one bird flying alone in search of liberty.

Even when we can't hear
The unthinkable on the dusty cities
Where love's cathedral is blasphemed
And forgivness smell comes from liberty
The bird flies in search of liberty.

Engulfed in the unlimited trust
Saddened we sniff the greatest romances
Through the books that foster time and kill forgivness
On behalf of a city of mortality we are preached all day
How this is worsening and declare ourselves as fools

## The Waist of Time

Today nothing beautiful happened
My calendar remained empty
Nothing bad happened
Expectation is drawn on a window
Cold expectation, like ice over our heads
And the dark swedish days
That turn to yellow our warm vision
Time crumbles quietly and its ruins swallow us.
In between our feet which have lost its equilibrium.
Time flows in the unknown sea by the furious river.
In the space are shaking the surprising looks.
And the heavy steel question marks wheighing upon us
Explode in the wirlwind time without mercy
Yesterday wearing thick sweaters has arrived and easily prevails, very quiet.
Mysteriously. Very similar to the unending tunnel.
No one knows how to enter neither knows how to exit.
Therefore nothing new today. The times are clashing desperately.
Saddness is waived without a word. While a lightning is discharged in the sky
Like a flag of blunders and time of sadness.
I am expecting the ruins of the overthrown time
As sadness is waived over our heads,
An unimportant news such as lightning,
Was on the newspaper everywhere. Sadness.
And thousands of readers grown in front of that nonsense
That doubles the bitterness of my expresso
Nothing bad today. Words stopped existing.
Hospitality on the window is unhappy like a night crow.

## Clashes

I bite sometimes my teeth furiously
My tongue remains on my teeth sometimes
With a neddle have to sew my tongue.
Some days have no desire to, my little angel,
Surprised with myself how I bite my dreams,
Fight with them until bleeding,
Bite them and clash with reality,
Over nights with autumn's dreams
And lovely smiles from spring
The hope for victory strangles saddness
I bite the days and nights all together,
Gloomy nights, nights close to dusk,
At times I am bloodened everywhere,
With my heavy, very heavy teeth
Heavier like the rocks of the highlands,
Sometimes the world sleeps at noon,
And there bows the myth of strength resistance
The world is completely confused and shaken,
Sometimes the world forgets the bowing of knees
Falls asleep under the sounds of children songs
Suddenly is dissolved from the bitterness affecting our intestines
Confuses the brain and the mirror image is lost
The tree of life covers the street in a morning full of Sun dew
And I, sometimes alone clash with the world
And become passionate on the nakedness of poetry.

## Small Steps

I measure my time glancing like a bird
That day when the Sun was sliding towards the west
A crow was parading in front of our eyes
And Earth stopped breathing from anger

Why wasn't possible to return the Sun
Right there when he first smiled to our sweet look
An I would pass the road up the hill with feathers

That day when my look dissolved
Earth was shaking from the cold

The Sun looked towards the Albanian Alps, as a sinful woman
The actions to stop his look were fruitless
My vision sunk completely under the Sun's eyes...

## The Shadow of Crows

In the island of cordiality solitude is bitter
And the broken structure of sex
In the river of time was crawling

I didn't recognise Homer and his blindness
With the steps of Achilles I measure the current time
And the kilometers beyond Ithaca

Your azured bulb becomes lost in the nudity
Of the dark night where your mind changes
Confusing acts of a shadowing spirit
Cold shower drops in the island of solitude
Fall on the cracks of your sex

The unwritten drama in the ruin's theater
And the icy kiss that burned the tearful bulb

In the day when I had confusing thoughts
One crow observed my smiling eyes
And the myth reflected under the shade of crows
The partial pieces of written art

Eyes are neither windows from the past
Nor are they doors to escape from sadness

## The Painting of Love

Mona Lisa was smiling
Her heavenly eyes speak of her immensely
Wetted, touching and soft
As special as they are incomparable
Her disheveled hair speaks of her
Were the land of passions changes its shapes
And the world is lost in front of her sad vision
Contracted like an open stage curtain
The world is small in front of her vision that burns
And greatly attracts on the mysterious world

Under her chin relaxes peacefully the world
And under the pressure of silence
Respirations are counted with inflated vains
Pressured by the numbness of time
Her mysteriously covered breast speaks
A mouthfull for the thirsty verse
And the many colors painted on those eyes
In order to challenge the perversity
Therefore, while smiling
Mona Lisa was bursting from love

## The Trial of My Poetry

The castle of justice cannot fall apart
With a wind blow from our mouth
Even if Joseph died miserably in the roads of Paris and
Prague
The process is not closed  and it remains as such
Great Fridays cannot be understood without great Sundays.
Poetry is innocent
You cannot take away her immunity even when she is naked

My uncombed beard,
Grown over the burning fires
You may never be able to kiss it,
Covered with freighning spiders

This poetry is boiling for love
You may kill her and place it in the grave
You will never touch her thoughts
Poetry is pure and spotless
Kill her if you want
And snakes will rise to bite your eyes

Mad cats will be running against the sad breasts

Kill her if you want
It will destroy the spirit on the grave.

## My Alphabet

Letters like stones are descending
On the alphabet with meaningless figures
A fragment of my life is turned into a cross road

Like in crazy dreams
I smell my escape towards inferno
My alphabet,
Poetry extends its meaning
While expanding its passions towards the sky
And passionate vocals exploding
Over my eyes
The irritation of solid letters,
Ruins the sleep of frontiers
In the universe of time without poetry

As a ragged man in cities of the world
Looking for advise from poetry writers
In order to understand the words from the stone
How it agitates the abstract thoughts

I am the steps and the road towards the land of poetry

In the road that reposes after every walk
Of ignorants dancing with a noise

The marathon of poetry over the burned souls
Raises the water just like Jesus Christ

## Illusion of a Word

In unkown horizons I recall my memories
Up to the smallest details

Connecting the words for illusions
My fingers arose just like rocks

The walls are built
With the sounds of the guitar
And the smell of forgiveness
Is nearing towards the illusion of words

As in bronx the feelings are suppressed through unknown horizons
In the bed over the grave
The register of love is endless
Only words are connected foolishly for illusions

## Ancient Story

From the truth the bugs of lies are coming out
While our feet lose their balance
From the turbulence of thoughts
In the cosmos of words they shook the repentance

An ancient story was never told for centuries
And for the same story fierce battles occurred
For many years we became tired from the shadows,
Like flags of defeat and fields of encounters
In which to find the traces of truth in the ruins of tears
Through the icy pedestrians where it's sleepery
The ignorant headed viciously towards the temple of madness.
Poor us, in search of the ancient story.

## The Multi-Colored Time

To search is as artful as kissing the Sun,
Oh, sailing through the abandoned night
From the naughty ass moon with dark colors
Oh lonely night with half blinded eyes,
Oh multi-colored time that is widely grown,
As a noose dancing over my head
Proudly shining her eyes just as cyclop's eyes
I could see how fast her feet move...
Is not Achilles but flies just like in ancient battles
Sometimes in America, catches saddness while dreaming,
Sometimes in Europe, anxiety catches her on the bed,
While in Asia, nightmare catches her on the road,
Sometimes awakes with memories from the horse,
Makes love in the fatal belly
And confuses the roads in front of her feet

The uncolored, nameless and unmentioned time
Although unritten dances with loud music
Wriggling like crazy just as a girl with high heels
As a storm that cannot stand metaphors and ironies
With irregular structures up to exception,
Walkes with a dissolved vision in the modern roads
And suddenly cannot find comparison among modernists
Neither from progressists
From professional ignorants with dictionaries of demagogery
That never undestand the art of silence
In order to suffocate the frightening noise.
My particular time in the engulfed globe
Baptized at night, nameless, and abandonded with loud music
With the shade of crazy crows
Is not similar to Vyrgil's time,
With quiet heroes and absurd wars.

It doesn't seem like the time of Christ, neither the time of Judah,
My time is never the time of Heracles' river.
Have to go through it, and sniff many times,
And to walk through the fat memory of spiders
And unmercifull warms that bite.
Nervously I have to disagree with Heracles,
At the same time have to take a shower twice:
In the same water and once with storming fire
Later with the art of silence and water of benediction.
Between me and the time flyies the spring bird
With cold feathers and frightened eye,
Touches the affliction drawn on top of the castle of thoughts
The kidnapped time from ragged people with snake skin,
My dear Dardania attacked from anti-time.
And the myth of forgiveness blossoming as a flower every morning.

## The Creation

God, created six days continuously
On the seventh day
Placed all the authors in the garden of secrecy
Taught them the skills and assigned their mission.
Since then only one thing remained a secret:
On what day of creation was the first drag of the snake, on
Earth's surface?

## As Usuall

In the morning my soul
And my bed is wet from tears
They take me back to the era of poetry
In my uncompromised war with metaphors
To learn how to dance with the wolfs

The greyish Wednesday is not today
Neither the big Friday
Christ is not crucified in the cross
Meanwhile the church's bells are ringing

My bed remained as a pawn
Widening through the space
In order to catch the star of welcome
And a response for many dilemmas.

## Drama

The black scarf on the heavy neck
And the suffering look
Dissolved the shining colors
And black requisitions take our eyes
A donkey screams as to deafning our ears
And the shadows of crows mysteriously
Bite the words of exhausted actors
A judaic kiss
Inebriate the actor named Miracle
Undresses the underware with a splash of piss
And the spoiled throws them in the public
The first act without orgazm
The game lasted several minutes
And the second act plunged in contemplation
A donkey moves on the stage many times
Two crows fly with their shades as water
The shy actor refuses to undress on the stage

While my drama perception was itching my eyes
Neither Godo waited like me.

## Compromise

Word inspires life
Sends messages
Even when it is quiet,
Don't guess for this
Look at poetry,
Every letter soaked with blood
Is hanged on its subject.
Trust the weight of life
On the word killed over the tongue,
Believe in metaphors
On the moulded word that boils inside the flower blossom
In the self sacrificed compromises
Through the cabinets of sighing lust
Grows and shortens many times my beard
Together with the tongue that keep the words together
Silent in the blossom and tied as a noose
Together with the thoughts that fight the walls of enclosure
The disconcerted castles in my eyes,
The snake with open mouth smells the humility
And I had to fall in silence
Under the compassionate compromise with metaphors
I was quiet until silence turned into noise
Again as for stuborness,
I was in silence until the song in my verses exploded
Silence was mad in the uncombed beard
Under the uncombed hair silence was burned.

## Marbled Memories

The day of poetry sunk, and from the dark hole of the horizon is returning,
The marbled memory stretches to the times of Divine Comedy,
Behind the weak steps through many barricades
My thirsty spirit remains in the shade for many secrets.

The time of naked passions is demolished while flying as crows
It wonders as a rainbow over our tired heads
In the universe of exploding thoughts sleepingly we become drunk
The day of poetry is going to return
Poetry rests assured in the magic shade
And it will never unveil the immunity inherited by God.

There is no Zeus on earth, sleep well and shake the dispersed time
Shake the lost human being through the confusing advertisements
And the era of nonsense through the noise from everywhere
Very saddening, there is no room for art, no time for poetry

Words and the heart all burn together,
In the horison of expectations is resting a metaphor on the throat,
It is breathless and cries without understanding its pain
I am resting in her buried lips and caress her

My calendar is dissolving
From the summer sweat that burn the forehead,
I have to kiss the thirsty verse,
Today my soul is not singing,
Instead of songs we hear foolish noise

Useless noise to produce many pressumptions:
Some times some places everything is on its place
Of course poetry... will have its own prosperous fate

## Appeal

Don't sleep Muse, open your bulb
And borrow me the voice of the song
I bow in front of you
Burning but I am not the flames
Muse, in the begging was the word
And the word was everything
Already there is nothing else
Besides the word and love
Show me the frontier of life and death
And the kingdom of poetry
In my city with frontiers and walls
Show me the kingdom of benediction
And teach me to become the word's desciple
Of the free spirited music
That dances continuously
Show me more
Because history is a mark in the foot
Written and rewritten
Through the vibrating fingers
To make myths
And a hill of lies
Therefore muse, sing with me
And the love that boils
In the metaphore of time
Show me my God
Because the Sun rises for the good and the bad
The fiery language is turned into a shadow
And my vision into the horison of reception
While returns its mind into yesterday
And observes the structure of time
In the point of tomorrow

## Lonely Poets

Yesterday I met with the poet of great loneliness
Through the road of the sky was absorbing the Sun
His head was wrapped with dreams
To avoid the exuberance of the verses

Yesterday I met with the poet of the great love
Through the road to the forest with unknows colors
His head was tied with the eyes of Eros
To avoid the exuberance of the verses

Yesterday met with the Poet of great loneliness
Through the dusty road was licking his own footprints
His head was tied with history
To clear all the lies just as the sneak's head

Yesterday met with the poet of great loneliness
On the lonely metaphors road
Was naked outside
To intoxicate the world on his eyes

Yesterday met the poet of great loneliness
With the calculus of his heart
Was untying the unknown clews.

## In a Technical Time

In a time of diverse equipments
The soul languishes beyond the meaning of essence
Poetry is breathless and getting even worst
While a black cloud passes mysteriously
Without looking it in our universe of shadow

The only thing communicating freely in space
Is covered by a concrete blanket
Cannot hear today, there is no time to hear,
The ears of technical time are shortened
Inside the rumors of life while walking

Only worn out here and there
In the time that lies like a shadow
And a large nothingness that agrandizes over our heads
Like a black cloud in the sky
Very sad!

On all sides no one is listening were are the sounds of the drums
Ears of our time don't like silence neither hearing
They want only to talk and make noise on all sides
Nobody listens, Nobody talks, Nobody understands

Don't know how this time can be called as merciless.

## The Autumn of Soul

Autumn is very suppressed
Flowers are falling,
The spines are nailed deep in the body
Spiders take your breath away
As the black darkness bites my lips
The spiders slam on my face
The tongue boils blood and the song is soundless
High in the sky the spines have blossomed
How bloody is the sky over this Earth
Autumn is very suppressed
His breath is taken away

## Voyage of the Verse

Today the Verse departed for a long road, without a begining nor the end,
He told me as I was embracing the smiling Sun
Meanwhile my expresso turned cold from the bitter look

The sky cannot be placed on one hand,
With hands full of passion
Because victory is a perception of the fools,

And it is mysterious for not being quiet
The feelings tied together are overthrown by poetry
The Verse walks, walks even through the blood,

In the overthrowing storms
On the burning graves
My Verse is the hostage of life
Was sunk in the lake of forgivness
And strangled the saddness

## The Song of Light

Edith, my love, What is the happiness of writting?
Tell me your thoughts, Throw away your silence,
If not is the extension of memory according to Jose Luis Borges,
Or relaxation with yourself and for yourself
In the obscurity of great loneliness,
Were the secrets of universe are scented
With the language of the unmentioned,
With the preserved uncommon things
Through the kneading trough cooked with nightmare
O my God, the art of writing
Imagination above the river of silence
Kills the times with the look of Judah

*

My Love, the time of silenced river is agitated
Noise is grumbling, the storm is unstopable
Presently I am preparing my departure towards the peak
It is inaccessible with the little steps
There is a symbiotic coexistence between the written art and the night's nakedness,
With the worried woman and the noise coming from far away
With the vivid metaphors attacking as a thunder the Earth and the sky.
It cannot hide nowhere,
The built city on the mountain top,
As a convincing desciple in word and light,
Walk adjacent to the light,
Convinved that the word was in the begining
From it was made everything and without it nothing happened.
My dear, the city of noise cannot help me,
Looking at the city with colors on top,

# NDUE UKAJ - ITHACA OF THE WORD

Encircled with wolf lairs that scream terribly,
Sneaks and large warms,
Nasty odors with the smell of death.

*

This is why, my little angel, this is an accompanied road
With mixed written and unwritten memories
With difficult songs for the screaming voice
I have to hurry to represent the time that I never knew,
To learn about things that I never lived
Differences of silence and noise
This is why I keep the candle of darkness with my heavy hands
The words are fighting in the burned forehead
Metaphors are struggling bloodily with intoxicated ironies
They fight and cannot stand each-other

*

I have no idea how to go away from light
Even though it is far away with kilometers, months and years
With many doubts your are saying - It may be centuries old:
What is the meaning of this for a verse
That walks with the wings of lightning
With the power of earthquakes
It has to walk, beyond seven fields and seven mountains

The city of light is encircled with spines that bite your body

With sneaks and emperors of defending the crime,
Traitors and untrusted, have their nests nearby,
Dictators screaming all day for democracy are there,
And the world's contrasts are seen just as in a broken mirror
Sluts and pimps are there
There are countless public houses, there is no art and books,
Only public houses with many colors
Were the nightmare of anti-humanity is grinded

Between them there are wide myths just as the dust in between my feet,
And multiplied legends surfaced as the mushrooms after the rain

*

Is a long road,
Very tiring but should be done.
All sections of it have many names,
Partial interpretations through the ruined teeth
From the spittle with a dust aroma.
Is no important, because walk has its own purpose.
Now is the time and have to take deep breaths,
To throw away and vomiting the dust inside of my stomach,
While walking was the garden of Eden,
The red sneak and the tower of Babel were falling
And many disgraced people dancing with their head on the sky,
Naked Eva was beautiful, and candour like never before,
Thin, smiling eyes and lips and full of desire to bite,
And a thick branch of a dried tree
Oh my angel, where were you to remind me the greatness of writting,
The endless metaphore in the flodded river,
The river flows and has its purpose.
Even the barricades of narrowed mind cannot stop his flow,
It cannot be stopped from the Sun's rays that burn as a charcoal,
Even from the burned Earth, thirsty for water
Were our encountered thoughts are tired and challenged

*

Oh my dear, I exhausted you in the quitness of the river of love
With the tiring prologue of the ugly metaphor,
However, please take the courage to listen to me:

In the road were this verses will go through,
A rusty part of my body,
May have remained in one of the corners of solitude,
I have to feel it, although it smells really bad
Don't worry, nothing is going to happen to our son Louis
He is immune from dirtiness, dust and unfaithfullness
Against all sorts of hungry myths,
He is immune my dear love
Even from dictators and countless lairds filled with wolves.

*

My dear, listen to my old and new pains,
And the freightening shout of the misterious artist, Oh!
Listen to the lute played by the artist with a heavy shadow over us
Listen to the beating of Earth's vains that erupts from the bones of the artist
Dogs were fed with him...crazy dogs and emperors of mortality.
Their art serves as decoration just as the slut's powder
Listen, an endless shower is nearing its head,
I have to stop, and take deep breaths,
To leave aside biographies thickened with blood
Because the birds will wake up in their nest of quietness and start to sing,
Let's return to our forest of secrets,
There we have our weapons, verses, our bread, thick metaphors with irony,
This is why, presently, our concerns will take a perfected direction
I have to speak and sing a lot,
In our universe our time has many verses,
It has ruined the global climate, my love, and jeopardized ethics,
And every day even less art,
Inexistence of God is cheered frantically

## NDUE UKAJ - ITHACA OF THE WORD

From lost crowds in the lascivity of time
My love, cheerings are everywhere that God is ours,
How sad my love, it is to kill the God of others.
Violenced kids, asassinations of all sorts:
Suffocated motives under the yellow look
And apocalips is not ready.

*

This is why I have to move the metaphor's overthrown compass
Towards the peak of the town over the valley of love.
And attentively accompany the verses:
This poetry, has no eyes, but it has to see with attention
This poetry has no lips, but it has to speak without interruption
This poetry has no hears, but it has to listen
The unsaid, quiet unknown desires
This poetry is voiceless, it has no melody,
It has to sing, and to be heard beyond seven valleys and mountains,
Days are fighting with each other
I am traveling with my art books and love,
Our son Luis may sleep under the dreams of playfull endless waters,
He has no reason to be sad,
Now you see, days are rotten, smelling dirtness,
I have to challenge the saddness of Achilles,
There is time to write for the undone,
Have a long road to do,
Still on the first step, but I will walk with the energetic steps of Achilles
With me I have bloody feelings,
Bitten thoughts from the cruelty of time,
Memories that produce, death, frightness, escape,
This is the unwritten Bible in the context of hell,
Nothing helps me understand how to enter the Purgator,

## NDUE UKAJ - ITHACA OF THE WORD

More over nothing makes me recognize the door of paradise,
Fighting with darkness, my love, a fearce fight,
Please undestand my battle, my love
I have to learn the road of Dante,
He did the longest journey in the World.

\*

Listen, carefully: in the door of paradise there are no guards.
Take deep breaths and fearcefully fight again with darkness,
I hate it. Want to through it away
My love, we have fought tirelessly with the unlawfull blackness.
You disagree with me, blackness is the calmness of the spirit.
You tell me, it is the bed of our lustness
There are no metaphors, histories and fables about the art of love
I kiss you softly...I even have to speak softly,
You left me walk on the light my love...
I want to spend this trip through the light
I have never trusted darkness,
This is not nonsese and surrealistic simbols
My love, don't step over the snake in the doorstep
Before I make my first steps,
He won't bite, walk as a dancer over his skin,
This way will avoid betrayal and the tree of death
After a few steps will find the tree of life
However our departure has to go through many chronicles,
And to learn many things,
Countless mysteries preserved on "our bible of silence,"
Above all, I have to undestand the confusing and undeclared items
The unwritten and the enigma that throws me towards the holy mountain
In order to show his faith in God
Abraham killed his son...

## NDUE UKAJ - ITHACA OF THE WORD

Oh, My love, I have to stop again,
I have to pause a bit, it is a long road,
My breath has run away,
I have to cross seven valleys,
Mountains, forests, with wild animals,
Empty roads from deviated mothers,
I have to answer the question:
Where did Abraham find his faith to kill his son for the faith towards God?
The eras, meet, sometimes are kissed and sometimes abominated
In the nameless time the men kill and the weapons shout,
Pain looses meaning

*

Oh God I have nightmares from these sad imaginations
What a big ocean is in front of my feet.
I have to walk through it.
How can't I be afraid of sea storms
His furious monsters,
From waves kissing fiercely the sky at night.
Time flies my love,
The concept of time has swallowed me in the waterfall of metaphors
Have to be armed from the infidelity of time,
Against those who ruined poetry.
This is why I begged you not to walk at night, there is no loyalty.
Time is bending, the bells are ringing over the church
Lets light a candle to save our love
You see how days are ruined and attacked on all sides
Lets inaugurate our lives and with it
Both our love and our trip.
Oh God, The world has a few Don Quijotes
It has a tremendous need for them,
My friend who is a poet, would have said

## NDUE UKAJ - ITHACA OF THE WORD

The dark Sun is not needed, We have no Sun glasses
My dear, time is calling for the celebrated rebirths
To confess in front of ourselves and our identity.

*

You see, my dearest love, there are clouds,
We should lay on our river of sleep,
To never touch our tomorrow,
Once the Sun comes up, will start our journey,
The road is long and we are accompanying the wind
We will prevail my love,
Once you close your eyes, the world relaxes on that vision,
I fight with the metaphors and bite the darkness
Once the clouds are gone, and the Sun shines our Earth
Will depart again for our journey...
The city over the mountain is waiting for us.
Let's walk, the city is immuned to ice, sikness and desease...

## Only Silence

My love...you asked me with a sad look
In the unknown place were our silence falls
...Just as a kid I fell in the arms of silence...
I shook until my eyes saw the fire...flames
On the sweaty hands of silence...
...I saw the unseen point of yours
Right there my love is the poet's metaphor that you will never see...

*

Softly whispered that silence is sweet.
Silence again, and scared you whispered,
I want only silence as it becomes soft
I fell on her arms and scrolled as a kid,
Until I saw with my eyes the fire under the hands of silence.
As always only silence and the sky as a refracted woman
Painted with the colors of the artist
The moon is shining and bringing some love
From time to time, it moves softly as in the blade of the sword
My head between noise and silence, where to go first
My love you see how my dirty beard is burning
You see, I should not bother the silence of the unkown direction
In silence I run in a tiring fashion
With my feet ruined and destroyed over time.
Is a difficult time for metaphors
The era of unwritten and never sang memories
My love, beyond silence I see sweetness
Specifically at the crack were silence and noise are separated,
It is untouched, is devine and soft.
Is far away! Before I decide for one of those,
Please, I have to ask, also in silence:

# NDUE UKAJ - ITHACA OF THE WORD

Tell me... should I kill silence or not!
To walk over her riverlike blood together with the sky
With the noise of sounds unheard before,
With the shapes of poetry unknown before
On the refrain of songs unsung before,
With the portrait of paintings unpainted before.

*

Tell me, my love, what is best!?
To kill or not to kill silence,
Uniquely beautiful, you told me while sleeping:
Those who trust in love are fortunate,
Because they have the countless treasures of Earth;
Lucky those who trust in love,
Because the countless treasures of the sky belong to them;
Lucky those kneeling for love
Because in every angle their vision is multiplied
Later you mentioned:
Lucky those trusting in love,
Because they belong to the Creator
For seven days out of nothingness created the world.
Rivers have an origin and an end,
My soul irregularly falls on their purpose,
And I never analyzed that purpose.
I have to pause a bit.

*

You should understand my love, I have to leave your lustfull breasts
And to jump at the wings of monologue,
There I have to find my unwritten time,
My time is very thick in there,
As a big spider the dust has layed its shoulders,
And a killing blackness nears a rainbow
And after every bite the snake raises his head
And the bitten apple remains dry inside the sins

## NDUE UKAJ - ITHACA OF THE WORD

All this has a suffocating smell,
Never seen on the hollywood movies,
Neither seen from my grandpa, great grandpa and nor by my parents;
Thus, somehow have to bundle and bundle well this topic
To wipe with the morning's freshness the legends and myths
Which are gathered as a whole cluster under my feet.
There are no alternatives, my dear,
I have to shake the dirty word,
It will have unpleasant smell and be poisonous, you have to be patient...
Or you may sleep quietly,
Again I will return in your breast
And relax in the quietness of the romantic river.

\*

Don't forget the river flows forever,
Even though his waves change
The shape, rhythm, and size.
Here we are, rivers flow and pour,
In a place, this is their purpose.
Scared, later disrupted silence, without answering me;
What should I kill silence or noise, my dear love
Your bulb as an angel touched the sky
You asked me with your sad look
In the unkown point: Were is your silence pouring?
Screamed at me during your unusual conversation
I did not respond, neither said a word,
Not even a look or a hug,
Neither a quiet kiss during silence's first vibration,
In the first hit that her image suffered.
And there I was looking towards you,
My love this is the poet's metaphone when you don't want to see him.

# NDUE UKAJ - ITHACA OF THE WORD

\*
And remember one thing:
Normal eyes cannot see in there.
You, as never before can't stop your curiosity
To learn why silence is necessary in order to say!
Those beaurocratic documents
Where the world did not know how to be preserved in registers
Where libraries save lies extending up to the sky
In countless absurd speeches and conferences,
In countless laws that blow your mind,
In the absurd ancient theater,
Were modern and ancient plays are worthless...

\*
In the most disturbing fashion we talked about the process,
Intertwined the unseen God and the magic seven days on Earth,
With the Creation:
Because what he said was a lifelong lesson
First was the word, then Adam and later Eva
A red lovely sneak between them,
Surprisingly was there, you understand?
This history that has a shivering analogy
Is heavy and cannot be carried over our shoulders,
And the process didn't stop, it still was a process.
In the roads of Paris or Prague a character died like a dog,
But don't forget, it remained a process and immediately was revived
Now I have to stop our unusual dialog,
Even our silence won't understand us, no-one indeed will,
Let's kill the noise then.
\*
I will return again nearby your breast, wait for me softly,
My love, I will return and will bow to the nostalgia of silence.

## NDUE UKAJ - ITHACA OF THE WORD

Because the big dilemmas, whether they are or aren't, cannot be solved with silence,
I need noise, and connected words with complex meanings
For the deaf ears and ignorant heads!
Now I am walking after the noise,
The delirious world runs like an endless marathon.
We the unimportant players, Poets, the beloved ones,
Are at the end, and is not important,
Please don't worry we are in a marathon,
And this is not an allegory for the stubborn,
Don't take it as a sarcastic humour or a joke.
Is the first time that I am scared, dont think I am fearful
I have fear, I feel it inside,
Just like I felt the softness of your body in silence, my love.
Nontheless I have to walk,
Have no time to wait, have to walk...
On the road there are many snakes,
Many cats run towards me,
Children abandoned on the streets, my love, there are even emperors of death,
There are dictators living to kill
There are many of these my love!
Even, wonderers who increase hatred through the sperm of the road,
There are sluts that ask me to drink with them,
To make love to the most craziest forms,
There are treasures and a lot of money,
I have to walk through all these turbulent images just as an alchemist
You should never distress, I will never fall in love in a desert,
Not even with the crazy romantic arabian women,
Trust me, never suspect the mission of words;
Remember that Penelope did not wait for nothing,
Even Odyssey did not search naturally without a reason

# NDUE UKAJ - ITHACA OF THE WORD

*
Here again, we are nearby the purpose,
We have a reason to celebrate our love,
Before I depart with open arms towards the purpose,
I have to combat the cold, the night will be ending soon.
Tomorrow I have to search,
Have to take off the skin of fear, to be naked.
A new day is born,
A few birds are knocking on our windows with heartbraking rhythms,
Don't become emotioned, very soon will return in the nest of silence,
I will depart as soon as the first Sun beams hit the Earth,
Towards the noise, across seven valleys and mountains,
Until the absolute silence which is known only to the mistery of irony
I have to walk a lot in the long Universe,
On roads full of turns, threats and challenges!
You know it my love, There are big horn devils, with uncombed beards,
Self declared prophets and antichrists, gentlmans and masters,
They all are present on Earth and near God,
Don't worry, metaphores will be my shield,
The feeling will be my weapons, The words will be my mission,
For religion will be love, for my courage is poetry...
Very soon I will energetically embrace you,
The first Sun rays fell on Earth and over this verse,
I have to say it is the end but not our farewell!
I have to go now.

## Memories are Broken in the Mirror

While twisting we were squeezing our teeth,
Gathered all our fingers,
Closed tightly our hands
As Autumn was kissing nature,
We were hiding in the nest of love,
Deep and even deeper my love

Alone with the wind as co-travelers,
Silence and the two thirsty bodies were enough
In order to learn the sleep of happyness
The flowing river and the lustful songs

We were looking confused how the times were kissing
At times with passion and sometimes with a wolflike hatered,
Inside the nest of love,
While we were learning the secrets of life

When times are blackened, the rain stops,
Nature is blossoming, The sky throws away the dark skin,
You wispered in my hear, Love only covered emptyness
We didn't know weather it was Monday or a tiring Friday,
We scrambled our fingers,
Tightly closed our hands
Through morning dreams without calendar
We learned the unseen dream
And smelled the sleep of love
Counted the intoxicating respiration
The undelivered whispers to the nest of love
The unpassed kilometers that were waiting our walk
And screamed as fools in the river of passions
As angels we were holding after the stars,
In order to reach the maximum,
We were twisting and squeezed our teeth,

With the glass of love at the top,
We gathered our fingers tightly,
Towards the tree of life and the river of love
This was our everlasting war, for the triumph of love.

## Nostalgia

My heart is sweetened
And your eyes
Quietly are slamming on the roads
Wait and only wait
Over the ridge on the valley of love
One cloud overwhealmed the Sun
The assasinated word won't be written with wet letters
Bitter irony won't stand it
I (don't) feel sorry for the unsaid words
Whether the warms are grinding or not
My heart
The time allows the smell in the dissolved thoughts
The colors of time have no flavor
And the stirring is here and there

## Becoming a Poet

*"Don't become a poet unless you won't die*
*For every word, and every verse."*
              *A. Shkreli*

I lived yesterday to become a poet today.
For a long time I dreamed
Through the lost night lost in the horizon,
In the dressed night with the muse's skin
Two thousand times recited the advice to the poet

Bloody in the dream with great saddenes bitting my verses,
Nails remained afflicted in the verses
The cup of enigma almost hit my forehead,
There, were thoughts are grinded for you,
Were the Sun fights with the endless vulcans.
On the dilemma's blade recited to myself two thousand times the advise of the poet
Cannot touch with verses the depth of Earth and the height of the Sky
For poetry the inferiors say that it is impossible to die for the verses,
Today I live for tomorrow....
To become a poet
To strangle, the biting blackness with candles

*

White rainy clouds are over Copenhagen,
There is no more blue sky
Some crasy ideas run through space
While the marathon of meanings weighed heavily in the cosmos

In the peaks of poetry were the sky meets the Earth:

## NDUE UKAJ - ITHACA OF THE WORD

Is not meaningless to walk through Hell and Purgator in order to reach paradise,
Were the usual eyes cannot see anymore,
Neither can see the blue eyes of thin swedish ladies

Only the bloody knees know how to walk forever,
And the eyes of Mona Lisa penetrate in the ancient castles
The strength in the walls of thoughts.

Some bloody stars are pouring like memories of times,
Pour very misteriously in the forehead of poetry.

Therefore to become a poet means,
To scream every time there is rain on Earth,
And everytime there is Sun Shine,
To feed with verses, to become a poet,
To have butterflies just as the birds in the sky
To touch so many depths.
To go in the hill of love,
Were the sky meets the Earth, to see what the world can't see.
Were is imposible to walk, to go only with bloody knees.

To become a poet means to trust in love,
And to fill the dry ocean with drops of water.

## The Candle

At the first day of the week
At noon the Sun was pale
Darkness swallowed our eyes
From the cellar came the candle
With his mold of wax

Lighted for brilliance
To strangle the darkness
Lighted for warmth
In a frozen winter
In endless darkness
In a night covered with the roaring of wolfs
The candle
Could not withstand the winds
Until everything turned into endless darkness

## In Hamlet's Castle

Going down the road of silence,
The heavy shadow Sun remained over our heads
The ship cuts through the stormy sea,
In order to touch the pretty pain
Over the steering wheel is Hamlet's castle,
Mysterious as it ruins silence
I see the sad eyes of Hamlet
Sweated from worrying,
I see the high walls were the cursing
From the sky is drawn
Were the eyes of treacherous mom,
Were intoxicated during lies
I saw Shakespear's suffering feet
And the world how it holds the dreams,
With anxiety and saddness altogether
In that castle.

## Six Letters

Six letters serve as a meaning of six days of creation
On the seventh day the Garden of Eden was a lustful bed for love
Eva did not loose the opportunity to undress!

The rivers are filled with six letters
The world walks in many directions,
With six letters you may find the meeting points
Even the valleys touching the sky can be raised further with six letters

Only with six letters is possible to harmonize the verses,
To sing uninterrupted, to spread the song as a Summer bird in many parts of the world
With the six letters can go above the clouds and in the deep blackness of Earth,
With six letters the world is gathered on one hand:
Love

## Black Time

Violated time
Memories are parading
As in the sword's blade walk without purpose
The marathon of ideas is stoped in the market of ideas
In roads full of beasts and heavy shadow beggers

Parade the memories just as invading soldiers
And running parades of treachery
In the innocent bulb
The color of time is deaming

Ideas are placed in the guillotine
And the sword is strangled
Unpaid bloody spots
Time is massacred
The days are dirty one after another
Time is dirty
And time in the forest
Is dehumanizing...!

## To: Father Peter Bogdani

How hard it is to gather all those mountains in your chest
And with one finger you grabbed them as a Rock

Truly was a Rock,
And over that rock was built everything
Then everything was destroyed
Besides your idea

A dirty dog that bite you miserably
Walks all day in Prishtina,
The city of Has is whiter than snow
And cannot be seen from Prishtina

The platoon of your ideas is digging the earth below our feet
Your rocky looks deprives us all
And are afraid because we still haven't tied the dog

Although, this concern, dear Father
Never was mentioned to us
After you passed with one breath the empire of death
And ruined its fearful sleep
Never told us how were you able to gather all the limbs
beyond seven mountains and valleys
And you sanctified the Albanian highlands
Never told us how you passed those mountains with just one step
To write history in rotten roots
On the heart of my land
Right were they offended you
And nasty dogs were fed over your body
And multifaceted temples surfaced from your bones
Dear Father, you never mentioned this to us.

## To: Father Gjergj Fishta

Father Fishta knew how to love,
To cry with the flowers of Fall,
With sorrow and bewilderment
To sing with the fairies of Spring
Father Fishta knew how to love until, sadness was inflamed,
And throw it in the sky,
He sang together with heroes and fairies
And swim like Dante at the doors of Paris,
From Saint Peter learned about his fatherland
Thus, only Father Gjergj knew how to sing with a slang.

## Mother Teresa

Your country inside the cosmos
Smells the suffering in every corner
And exceeds the iron frontiers of hunger
While assembling every idea available
Because the world cannot be invaded without weapons

With Albanian generosity
Your look of an earthquake
Similarly
Kissed the pain and hate

Built with love the everlasting castle
From the tears of the poor everywhere

You watered the times and dry flowers
In every angle of the Earth with a drop of water and little bread
While baptizing for ever the word Albanian

## Anton Pashku

Oh, one star fell from the sky,
It fell on the shores of the cruel sea,
It burned in a blink of an eye.
One star,
Oh, what a freightning scream,
Screams the cold sky.
Wearing a thick skin,
Earth is thundering heavily,
With the nervous echo of the sea
Oh, what a deep mysterious sigh,
Very sad and very sweet
Hidden, together with centuries saved in forgiveness.
Oh, everlasting mystery,
Unexplained screams
In the heart of the mysterious artist,
Cannot understand this clamour,
This engulfing outcry
Without counting centuries in our fingers,
Without describing loves with detail.
The naked women and the quietude
As the forbidden apple are bitten,
The sneaks scrolling in the roads of our capital,
And the planted tree scrolling in the bridge of life,
While the dry trees and molded earth shouted Pashku,
Only once as a testament...

## To: Ibrahim Rugova
*Ancient Dardania*

When we begged to hear the skin of Ancient Dardania
Wrinkled and grounded
Forgotten through the dusted centuries
We did not know about Flori and Lauri
Not even for the dream of resurrection

If you learned a lot
Let's make the rocks and concrete hearts to cry,
The stone to cry, to make them cry
With their tears to water the forgotten centuries
To whiten the dark times, to whiten them all
To plant the tree of life
My prince, when were you asked to wear the skin of ancient Dardania
Through your feet pulled your underware
And touched with your hand the forgotten centuries
You tied the centuries tighter and even tighter
and walked with the devine star...
The dust of darkness was shaking only shaking
We were breathless
A, we heard from your lips:
Threw away your underware under the feet,
Because this place is sacred
We were saddened from the magic silence of the ancient dreams
Saddened from the long night
For promises of the promised land
The song quickly crossed the mountain, fields, the sky, even the birds were singing it.
The birds together with the sky and the fields
And our voice turned into an orchestra
we were walking and listening the heavy weight of words
Dardania, our sacred land,

## NDUE UKAJ - ITHACA OF THE WORD

The sweet sounds of your song and words are magic
We walk in a sacred place

When the smile would fade
We were shaking in anxiety
As Jesus Christ you taught us every Friday the prophecy of resurrection
Learned on dust and darkness,
We had no light
Neither for the song of love
Gave a spirit to every moment, with a spirit filled our times
Including the forgotten centuries, and the saddened centuries
Engulfed deep and even deeper with the freightened spirit
The transformed history was facing cruelty
Walking and walking in the open through the fire

That day when death kissed your lips
Your song stopped in the tip of your tongue
In Dardania turned into tears
Fields, mountains and many more were crying
Your smile was crying, the shivering belching in the sky
The refrain of the song was crying, crying with a great solitude
Because no one could sing like you
The shaken dust of centuries
Was not living
Neither the wrinkled Dardania
Only sacred words, sacred blessing and stories: Dardania is Sacred
We saw your dream shaken from death
It was sang triumphantly
Not only fom those singing in Illyrian

That day when death kissed our lips
We lost our Sun, and his warmth
That day when death was caressing your lips

In every corner we heard the voice of your song
Washington, Brussel, Vatican, London, Berlin:
Every where Kosova, Dardania, is our sacred place
That day when death kissed your lips
And Dardania was sunk into tears
The sky was dark
How marvelously you joined all your loved ones, that you always mentioned
The Great Skanderbeg, Pjeter Bogdani, Mother Teresa, Pope John Paul II
Deep inside us we were shaking and wiping our eyes
As your song was always present:
After the Friday of death comes the Sunday of Resurrection
Triumphal you declared survival but now with dying eyes
Poets were speechless, surprisingly speechless
The birds were singing your refrain, but no-one could sing it like you,
Resounding, highly resounding:
The bird was singing well how to love our Ancient Dardania, our very sacred country.

## The Poet
*(To Rifat Kukaj)*

He is as an oracle,
Turned the pieces into one,
The entire objects turned into pieces.

Sang for the kids, was made a kid.
Sings for the sky, turned into love

The poet was praying and sang like Jesus:
Allow the kids to come to me, because only those are the owners of the divine
With the teachers' magic skills,
With the voice of Oracle, turned into chorus

The poet is singing very sweetly
Even when lamentation is on earth, and the sky throws poison and is sad,
Yes, this is the only song of the poet

The poet sang, very well sang, with great joy
Even when the sky was crying
Even when Earth was exploding from the veins filled with blood,
Even when, children could not play the game of magic childhood,
Also when mothers were crying in the fortified forest with the babies on their hands...
While walking

Writer Kukaj was singing,
He loved the song,
He loved the verses,
Rhymes,
Rythms,

Question marks

The Poet was singing
For Angels, and Demons,
For ancient songs,
For the Albanian nostalgia
To the clean blood,
For the spring like ideal.

## The Mother's Voice

The voice of mom is sweet,
Is the quiet relaxation of untouched dreams
Is sweet just like the Summer birds with magic melodies
There are shining the deep eyes of the World,
As an earthquake love explodes
Love shines with continuous Sun rays
More distinguished, more reiterated
Oh, Mother's voice is so sweet
Together with the melodies of the mornings of life,
Together with the pronounced and mispronounced alphabet
It is sweet, the voice of mother is very sweet
In the blossoming valleys of the Spring
Under the kiss of the first Sun rays
Of the ups and downs through the bloody knees,
My mother's voice is so sweet.

## The Kiss of the Star

A little light after darkness
Only for one moment
There is the sad look
The beloving eyes
And needless thought

A little light
Just to kiss the burned star
Killed with your look

Just a little light
To embrace the fiery sky
Just a little
And to die with my look towards this poetry...

## Thirst

Beyond seven valleys and seven mountains
A thousand times whisper the word freedom
Surrounded by malicious spines
The frontiers impossible to pass with tired feet
Sprained from the contracted heads,
And cruel shadows with a dirty beard
Hanging on walking sections
Today beyond a thousand hills and mountains
Beyond a thousand memories
Listen to my voice with a different color
While it sounds with sorrow
The universe of dreams
Together with the time when one world is together

Freedom,
We strangle pain
While hiding our look
In search of the road towards the structure of spirit
To rescue the respiration...

## Sickened Memory

Kill the sky
With a lightning attack
To be buried on Earth
Don't help it
Even the Earth throw away
On its intoxication behold the blood
Gather the bones
And build the walls with prostitutes
Do everything
Devil has exploded on the eyes of the world

Crazy cars run over my chest
Just as in a marathon of existance
And you don't have to worry

Don't misunderstand and don't worry
Everything is normal
To kill a nation
To ignore a nation
Do everyting because nothing is absurd today
Neither for the life with no head
Neither for the Head without life
And frozen lamentation on the lips

## Taboo

Yesterday you talked nervously to me with the elements of
fear growing in your lips
Just as the morning Sun
Never love the love when you can't change the meaning
Discouragement boils just as the water on charcoal

You are speaking today engulfed in the sleep of silence,
Like never before with the values of trust just as the morning
Sun
Suffer for love in order to change its meaning

You see how the question mark is changing its function with
an exclamatory mark
I kiss the ideas inflamed with each other
And poison the negative dreams
Just as the contrasts of the world we continue to see

## Philosophy of Foolishness

This watch is crazy
In the wet paved roads with tears
With crazyness narrates logic
Philosophy of foolishness
The naked topic resigned from egoism
And is slamed in the dirty windows
And the motives are connected
After the esthetics of the killing metaphor

Days are rotten one after the other
They smell awfully
I am sunk with Homer
Sing the tragedy blindly
My existence was cut with my shoulders

The privileges of crime are grown
Logics born from privileges
My axle is cutting right were it hurts

With the grey grass and thirst for words
Comes the wind and with the nasty metaphor
Words from metamorphosis
And later comes rain, storm and Sun
The dust of sadness
And deceptions
The art is predicting
The rising of the aesthetics of fate
Today my axle is cutting were I left off
Yesterday it opened my field and today opening its road...

## Welcome

Grabbed the welcome
The closed window
Its hopes from anxiety
And placed them in my soft hand
It spoke
And
Was confused on the gramatical conjugation
Today
Tomorrow
After Tomorrow
Again warm welcome
The window was closed
An Oak threw a black shadow
And welcome was painted by my hand

## A Tragicomic Scene

The Sun winding through the icy sky
Over the hills are walking the mountain witches
The pale words are dropping in the torn pages
And a poet in the flodded pedestrians
Is fighting with his metaphors

Inside the mountain is screaming the word
Ideas swimming in the lakes
To express the troubling times
The rivers of blood
The broken crosses
The bones turned into dust

No-one is trusting
Big heads and deaf ears
Neither for massacres nor for violence
My verse is boiling in a page of dust
The Balkan peninsula is burning as the blood runs in rivers

## The Kiss

Made a noise to silence
The bodies were shocked
The words were silenced
The hearts were inflamed
The Sky and the Earth cannot embrace
Neither extinguishing the star with fingers
The Sun beams cannot be stopped through the sky
Neither the moon to brighten the morning can't be stopped
The longing cannot be extinguished with nostalgia
Neither languish cannot be separated with tears
Only the lips are burning together
And throwing fire away

## The Aesthetics of Love

Your hair was flowing
Over Prishtina was raining
Your hair was shaking and twisting
As the waives were storming,
Indeed just as the waives of the sneaky sea

Between time and kiss distance was running like a bird
The thoughts were accompanied by the wrestling leafs,
And the deep thinking steps between time and kiss
The shade with a rocky silence proudly was standing

From the passage of the movement of feelings
To the perception of desire
It was as long as many centuries
Inside the drunk music's earthquake
You breathed the air in a erotic fashion
On the Spring, vivid birds sing in the sky
Together with the gladness of happyness,
When your hair was shaking,
Earth was shaking, the Sky was shaking,
And I became crazy
I was stunt
Was trying to explode
Just as lost in fire was searching
The Love
And your hair
And the astonishing lips
Even capable to extinguish my life over the cries of your lips,
On the last drop of blood to strangle thirst
And to write love as the last word
*
That day everything could have been real
Time would brighten and to slam the eyes

## NDUE UKAJ - ITHACA OF THE WORD

Deep in the sky the shadow of the painting seemed Mona
Lisa was waiting
Everything was real during this particular day,
Transforming the sky into love
The sky would be as a romance
Far away to smell the wall of feelings
And to navigate towards the sky, my angel
To kiss the sky like eyes with...
Until falling asleep over them
Like Ikar, I am running towards the sky
Thirsty, and badly burned
Extinguish the nostalgia
While lost inside,
Filling the love while dying in it
That day was only a blue Sky
And I was extremely loving you...

## Dilemma

I have said that mountains are guarding untouched secrets
I have said, many times...that the bottom of the sea cannot be touched
I have said it and repeat it again that Poetry is not a disconcerted joke,
Neither a bitter humour to wipe out faceless roads

Absurdities have never been and will never be art decorations
It is better to sing and sing non-stop,
Rather than screaming every time the Spring disappears with tears on her chin,
To be blind from troubles that vanish just as the frost from the Sun
And to kill the black defeat in the turbulence of the dilemmas
With the bitter look in the forest of dilemmas

## A Song for the Song of Love

In my desk full of memories a white page is flapping
And shades guarding my verse in the marathon

The whiteness of this page swallows my eyes
Attached from the aroma of nailed time and the passion for a little color
Which is waiting to ruin the symetry of welcome

Imagination is surrounding shadows
Tied together as an erected penis on the naked legs of the seven miraculous days
The song of love is a ballad full of echoes
Nostalgia, eyes, lips, intoxication and sighs
Trembling and strangling in nostalgia

Imagination that confuses the World
Has given birth and mortified your naked breast

And poetry remains the element of wonders which raises the world on a blink of an eye.


It is nonsense, this white page is scratched
Without a meaning and not writing songs for you
The memory that burnes flames has engulfed this lines.

## Dialogue

Talking means to live

The game of imagination is stunt and looses its rocky patience
The silence wearing thick clothes can be met in the first circle
Its shade with a naked solitude can be met in the second circle
On the third solitude is standing as an ancient castle
Its sound echoes as in ancient battles:
For silence and hearing we always fought
Even though never understood whether listening was silence
Or in the context of devil silence meant listening
I don't know it here even today and tomorrow
Nervous spiting the time and the tall ruins
Inspired from forgivness crowds are screaming
words always have no meaning
The uncombed ideas mislead our spirit
The unsaid pretend to be big
Until the artist die together with sick crows in the storm
Here there are no big words
Crazyness can never have logic.

# NDUE UKAJ - ITHACA OF THE WORD

## Today ...

And today the verses disappeared
The time of poetry dissolved
Fucked with the evening sluts
The musicians with uncombed beards
Kill the lonely silences
Guitars keep the rhythm
The history raises lies
Lies raise History

And if you want to know which is my love
Take the sky in your hands, count the stars in your hand
Together with the dust, wine, grappa and the çifteli
Grab the Earth and squeeze her blood from the vains
If you want to know who is my love,
Throw away the look in the crazy nails located in the hands of Jesus
If you want to know who is my love
Shake your heavy sleep as the bear

The cruel soil opens frighteningly
The life is circling as a ring,
First walking one step forward,
And we are smashed two steps backwards
Our life circles as ring and searches the shores
The wounds are swimming and swimming
Inside the books of history
Pissing, poisoning over the head,
Red and black sneakes,
through the wound
Of the cloudless lightning
To the compact Earth explodes blood on its heart
Many times tied with the head are screaming
Blood is falling on the eyes of screaming drums
Eyes are like mirrors were times are broken and galaxy

relaxes,
Wounds are swimming from the sky into the sea,
My bewildered metaphore is exploding towards the depth
And if you want to know which is my love:
Strangle me with fire and keep me alive on fire
Fill my stomach with fire
Let the Earth burn from fire
Let the sky be covered by fire
Let my head and my brains
Become fire

## Save the Tears

Save the tears
Time is measured with the decorated immagination

The blind Homer was breathless into tragedy
After he sniffed the lustful bed of Helena

So don't get tired to become a poet
Love sings without voice
Even embracing the soft neck without tied hands

Save the tears!

## Failing

With millimeters I measure the words
Through the hands of the sinful poetry is languishing
Don't blame me my dear,
I made you tired with meaningless metaphors
With these verses from cloudy weather

The word connected with the dirty forgivness
Of dismantling the roots
Were the leaves are growing just as in the Autumn tree
In order to enclose herself in the forgiveness of winter

Through the aged solitude
My step as big as the sky
Frightening forgiveness
In the roofs with snow

Singing for nothing to our ancient song for the aged songs
It is nonsense for the vivid heroes to shrink in the modern verse
And for nothingness placing a meaning to the verse
The depth is dissolved without recognizing the essence
In the forgiveness of winter that freezes your teeth
Ballads, together with legends, myths
And the fairy spirit
They all placed the bride in the wall softly,
And kept her breast outside just for love
The books of the organic roots are unbalanced
Cannot use the stomach of the Trojan horse
To escape from the convoy of destruction
Baptism's formula is suffering
In the shrinked Earth every Spring
The road through Hell is shorter
Than the saddness from failing

## Succumbing

My beard is burning
And my tired feet
Cannot get anywhere

Smoke and its fog hits my eyes
Unrecognized noise comes in my ears

The book of my history
Is burned together with Troy

My dear friends
Somewhere in Shkodra the traces of escape
Are painted with a grey color
No one is willing to touch them

We never could learn
The History under the shape of Evil
Although Father Zef Pllumbi told us:
Dante has written the new Comedy

We are cold and disappear from the Sun
We don't have black glass to defend ourselves – is
screaming Ali Podrimja

We get drunk under the literary parades
Interpret as we wish
We cannot listen the metaphores cut in the throat

Over portraits are pissing the crazy dogs
As we are told to pray in the temples of lies
The wish of God!

We never learned the language of Fishta
And he provided us with the big voice as a storm

Tragedies dancing over our heads

And over our heads portraits are expanded
Are bitten under the silence of anxiety
While we are quiet
We should twist crazyness as a child

This is not Kafka's time
While there are kings without kingdom
And absurdities arise as flowers in the garders

Intellectuals selling cabbages
Academicians begging help and food
Every day Migjeni dies young
The tears of Mother Teresa passing as graves over the stones
The disgraced people have forgotten the sanctification with water

## **Autumn Night**

It is cold. You see my love, My heart has fever,
How is languishing the bird's song
After the Spring of Love

It is cold my love
The inflamed language cannot help
I have fever and high temperature in my heart
Although don't want to abandon silence,
This nest of pleasure
And, you should not underestimate the songs of the happy bird,
After the Spring of Love
In this deep Autumn evening
Were there is no light, fire and tears,
Only a little love
The gigantic solitude is crowling as a big spider
In the dark corners of my existence
You should be careful and don't cry
Don't sing any unheard songs
Don't sing any unsang songs,
It is worthless no one will listen them

My love, night and day are clashing
Are embracing while kissing in their foreheard
For the departure of no return
The world is dying in your eyes today
The blossoms of the Spring have the aroma of your neck
The devil runs away, escapes away
As a broken sound of the unintentionally cracked guitar
In the forest that swallows you with frightening scream
The times are passing and clash with each-other
Only the terrible dreams remain in the memories

## Your Fate

Crawling through the rusty rings
Killing the sleep in silence
Your fate is my fate
I am not a prophet neither Christ
I trust in love
Which silences the world
Which brings the world to its knees
Verses and the love told me
That I am born when you die

## A Wound

The colors of contrast have kissed my walking verse,
Through the dusty road with splashes of rain that were throwing blood

And the red color is no more red
Roads with spines and rotten times
With a chocking smell.
Dreams are noisy as they leave
And collided as stars while loosing their mind

The dreams cannot separate the inflamed wishes,
Neither the frozen nights when your mouth is shaking from the cold
The tears are touching and crash over the burned pavements
I am drunk with a glass of wiskey
And my emotions colliding with the mixed colors in my eye are drunk
The red is no more red, neither the sky I can't see
I see the longing as a song attached with the sky,
And I see every smiling morning the pale face
My wife likes poetry but can't write
However she learned
How sad when life is attached with pain
In every evening when we recall our lost days
And great saddness like pain is attached with death
Whispered the verses through the dream:
We are not separated by dreams
No one and never
Neither the sky cannot separate,
Neither God, Angels and Demons,
We sing the song of eternity

With graves and wounds in bed
My love for you never was old

Always suffering to keep it fresh
And you were born to stay always young
I sing for your my life
For the fiery longing
For the spirit that goes in eternity

## The Meaning

At the bottom line what is the meaning of art my dear
Through my fingers is changed your look
And Babel's calendar which was torn appart at his tower
How to decipher the unsaid and the unwritten,
And to understand absurdities as watered flowers

The arena of sweet thoughts is disrupted
Unimagined sinfull people running after the memorials of glory,
Day and night screaming without shame under the shade of pain
That screams frighteningly
The hydra screams for the sea
We kiss without knowing its benefit
And are loved unaware of consequence

My God, with what kind of shameless they are walking towards hell
Dressed with a sneak skin to improve their apparence,
Some one is stinging and others are being stinged

The caricatures of death kill the brains
While the unending mystery is heavier:
A bitten apple grows rotten teeth at night
Black sins cannot hide during the day
And their existence of defeat

Is unknown in which day of creation the snake scrolled towards Eden
Also we never learned his mission

## In Search of Lost Vocals

In search of lost vocals
My dear, I suddenly found myself inside the past
With my heavy fingers
I was gathering thick memories throughout time
Gathered the voice burned by lightning
And ideas were twisting in my feet
Just as crazy women in bed
As an Alchemist in the restless desert,
Walk through the wounds that hurt
With my tired hands
Gathering pieces of love
Together with hopes
The pain
Solitude
And nothing more or less
The passion to build the word's statue
Is beating inside the book covers that are closed by time
Closed by thirst for the unkown
And transmission of words.

## Love in Darkness

Darkness covers the space,
The unmerciful black night
With great power swallows the light

Inside the sky and mushy Earth
Shining as a lit candle,
Which the wind is flowing but impossible to extinguish
Just as your hair is flowing
Spreading
Over your shouldes as the sea, indeed truly as a sea
Love is born by tranquility
A million thought and one name
Run excited through memories
While your soft hands
Like angels
I feel them softly surrounding my neck
lost in a delirium
In that night when the light sparkled for love

## New Purpose

Even in dreams I am writting verses
In the pale mornings with lightning and smell of rain
I do the same when the sky explodes and the Earth is cold
And covered with blankets watered with sperm
We gather the passions that explode
Between my feet that are shaking
And the desire that makes me crazy

When the Sun falls into tears, he smiles as a kid
The motive of love secretly smashes the poetry

While I am having poison
Day, night, I strangle with the scarf of love
My divine poetry

## The Roots of the Tree

We walked through the bitter road
Just like in the garden of Eden
And the snake was leaving his shade in the word's tree

Just as God created us then
Together with Adam and Eva
And the seven magic days
Together with the first love and hate
We changed the shape of bad time until becoming sad

Many sighs of joy are loudly speaking in my verse
Many confusing desires are shaking until they completely die
Oh God, My angel, how to suck from the roots of the tree
Its liquid
When the word choked up in my tongue
And the sounds dissolved on the throat

There in the blue sky, is and is not!?
Together with the sounds
And with colors
Eden faded
And the great word: Creation

## Apocalypse

Confused ideas are appealed today
In the cellars of concrete
Without feelings
In the series of lies
The sinful of history
The architects of suicide
And to the partitioning of my existence
Impose projects
In the hut of slaughter
In order to have wolfs and sheeps
To live together
The exclamation point has changed meaning
The Antichrist is appearing rapidly
In the pedestrians with a noise...
And the psalming of Apocalypse
Just as in ancient Rome

## Tragic Aesthetics

Even when the sky reflects
How the Earth has fever
Becomes crazy from his wounds and pains in bed
The Dilemma is bigger than the pain weighing as the Sky

Even when the sky is shouting
Earth has pain
and the blood
Is drunk to extinguish its thirst
The World shakes the Dilemmas as much as the enormous mountains
And prays to become a dream
And to lie and confuse our eyes.

## Eclipse of Life

Deaf Night
Our theater is endless
In the choir of saddness
Violence from centuries
Transformed history
Are resurfacing
Projects are done by the ignorants
Projects are destroyed by ignorants
Regions,
Enclaves
Separation
Discordance
Today ignorants have surgery
Remain ignorants
To love endlessly is the propensity of God
And the breadth of love
The flattened spirit of the word
And of the gold of pacience
Our father in the sky!

## Perfected Time For Genocide

Kingdom of absurdity is born
Heads like pumpkin in the pile of affliction
Dance together with the wings of pain.

Preaching on the roads as fools strangled from dust
And a black cat runs intoxicated
While the forest looses its look in the eyes of women
And the Earth is filled as a painting with eyes

Time cannot heal the wounds,
If the revolt does not have the teeth of the wolf.

## Arguments of Time

Beyond every human look
Is hidden the politeness of the dirty moral
Everything is argued
Words are measured with milimeters, My God
And from here with dirty facts
The Song is judged,

With absurd notions,
The unspoken thoughts and the time
Which I have to carry in my hands are analyzed
Is not the time of Goethe's field
The spirit is not sold for wisdom!

## Fatherland

I love you beyond
The bloodened and wounded words
With pain and graves in my shoulder,
I love you more than words

It is hard to translate your sweetness
Your death and rebirth
Without maps and borders

Fatherland
Memories for your freedom as a charcoal are burning
To kiss you countless wounds
And your desires sucked by rotten worms just as a sponge

The selected words don't have huge meanings
Because I am terrified,
Poetry cannot afford the translation of your sufferings

## Love

The notions of love are gathered inside my eyes
Were the feeling is focused as a bird during a storm

The rebelling love against the malicious
A name that makes you swim until you are sunk
It unties the body and soul in the quiet river
Were the Earth and sky are kissing with lust and energy

Love does not recognize reason neither big words

With gurgling requests layed on my body and soul
For Love I am drawing my eyes in the tabloid

## The Kingdom of Straws

With the burned tongue over the fire
As a drunk I am controling my look
The kingdom of straws is bordered with Troy,
However is missing something,
 And that is, God
The paradox of the soft life
And the bad road to Ithaca
Cannot afford the small steps

Had Prometheus been alive
There would have been foolishness without salt

## Kosova

The evening cuckoos were singing over the sky
For years I did not understand their song
Neither I did not get what was the meaning of freedom
In the most ferocious meaning of the word
I lived its cruel weight

Kosova
The freedom in your sky never came
For your bad luck it even changed the meaning
And its border saddly was a terrible war
Meanwhile its shape turned into the colors of affliction
With a sponge are pulling our desires
Until soldiers dance over our heads
And upon us was imposed how to dance
Under the barrel of the gun
And naked women pissing over our heads
Remained scared
Kosova
Neither Achilles could not describe your tragedy

While my skull is eaten by dogs
And remember when my words were burning in fire
Only had I mentioned the word freedom

## An Evening in Dubrovnik

Under the evening quietude is laying quietly
The gigantic Sea is sleeping tumultously

Sleeping and shaking the unknown mysteries
Undressed with the frightening sounds
It highly looks as a lustful woman
Were the world discovers the mysterious dreams
And awakens under the sweats of saddness

The sea is sleeping
Its blue color engulfing my eyes
And I am lost,
Together with my history which from here has one of its limbs

## The Soul's Migration

My Soul migrates with no purpose
Through the burned beams
Runs without a reason
Through the blade of the sword,
Were history was rubbing
Just as in the hands of the ancient horseriders

And the unfinished story
While searching something lost
Forgotten and neglected
From the iron boots,
The heel stuck in the mudd
All this pain digging our brain

My soul migrates without a reason
Runs with no meaning
Through the blade of the sword,
Were history frictioned
To search the limbs
In the inflamed time
In the forgotten conscience
And in the river of tragedies
Were all these turned into a sea

## The Metaphor of Legend

Wounds are swimming on fire, earth and sea
The sister of Gjergj Elez Alia
Is dancing with her burning handkerchief
Music heals the wounds of her brother.

Legends are colliding with the rocks
Over Rozafa saddness is screaming
And Gjergj's Shadow over Adriatic
Ruins the dream of Hydra

Heroes are suffering
Earth and the Adriatic are suffering in flames
From the dusty books

The deprived Earth is cracking
Just as surrounded life is behaving,
We walk one step forward,
And then crash two steps backward

Life is just like in a ring
Is looking for a way out

Wounds are swimming
Inside the covers of history books
Pissing and poisoning over head
The red and black sneaks

The wounds are swimming
From the lightning without clouds
Blood is exploding to the cruel Earth

Head and times are screaming and are tied really bad
Sounds of drums are hitting our eyes

In the mirroring eyes were time is cracked and the galaxy is relaxed

Wounds are swimming in the sky and the sea
My confused metaphor somewhere deep explodes

Your face has two images
After this time comes another time

## Temptation

The exhausted time is tempted here and there,
It is hard my Lord to keep it straight
The wind of silence shakes it as a cherry leaf
The World smiles mysteriously
I am not worried my love
I am inside my own temptation
Were the soil is slippery over our feet,
Were the possiblity to keep my body straight
Is smaller that the big Zero

Temptation is holding my head away
From the crashes between the sky and Earth
For the sweet word just as the mother's milk
For the letters of my name that were swallowed by the lake of Shkodra
Many dirty worms fed by the vomited waist of alcohol
In the walls of Rozafat's Castle a woman was crucified
And twelve males were fakely swearing in
Thirty three empty bottles
I try immediately thirty three full bottles
Affliction explodes and screams:
- How good it is not to read poetry-
This means, simply, not to worry for anything,
Only lonely poets know how to love,
To love and love endlessly,
To grasp the Sun on the palm of their hands,
And to embrace the sea in its profoundity
Only poets know how to count
Your languishing silence
Our Shkodra, our glorious Shkodra,
The bloodied kisses from Kosova,
Ancient Dardania and the crucified top of Stubëll
And one common name:
To live in order to confess eternal misteries

## NDUE UKAJ - ITHACA OF THE WORD

\*
How to learn to write the future on the slippery soil
Under our elastic feet,
Goes frightened, goes in a blink of an eye
Were to steal a water drop and to aggrandize it as Christ
To make it bigger and turn into sea


Is thirsty from the chocking smoke
And to liberate the jailed thoughts

Oh my God, the skin of the ugly sneak
Raises his head night and day
Crolling in the breathless Earth

And a bunch of drunk reptiles
And an apple planted without love
In our garden destroyed accidentally
From the dust and spiders

Wow, How could it burn without fire and smoke...

## We Are All Odyssey

Searching is an art!
We are all a little Odyssey,
Some search Ithaca and some search Penelope
The Body parts: Limbs, eyes, ears
Were lost in the nakedness of the swirling water algae
In the blue and bitter Sea.

In the shores watered by millions of water drops
Are searching and will never return,
With the silence of Sea, with his noise
Is broken the most freightening silence
To search is an art the same as kissing the Sun with icy lips
To touch the sky by hand,
And to squeeze and drink his sweetness

Lost eyes in the sky and in the sea
The sacred place of Ithaca never was destroyed
Penelope defends it with cleverness
Hidding in the mistery of welcoming,
With big and black eyes,
Odyssey with blue eyes never stopped his search,
Searched and did not stop until the new return

\*\*
We are all a little Odissey,
Some search Ithaca and some search Penelope
In the Earth's labyrinths we are searching irrevocably
Until the bottom that is never seen
Some search Ithaca and some search Penelope,
The noisy and drunken World is waiting in the overwhelming music,
Everyone has a piece of Penelope in their heads
We all search a little and expect a little,

## NDUE UKAJ - ITHACA OF THE WORD

The walks have one purpose,
Away from the jailed night in the silence of sadness,
Some walking fast, and others with bloody knees
We are all walking, with great desire walking,
In the road of exploration, without rest walking.
Suddenly in a blink of an eye,
Our desires are strangled,
Sometimes are attached just as stars thrown in our forehead
Many times we step with heels over lost time,
And in other occasions we have them in our forehead
We are all a little Odissey,
Some search Ithaca and some searching Penelope

## The Art Of Love

My love, the night is falling,
Your eye is thirsty for sweet kisses
Extends its lust up to the sky
Sleep confortably in the river of love,
The Winter has taken off its heavy clothes,
– There is a warm Spring-
Your are not cold as always
Your Spring and your body
Allow me to give you many kisses
To loose my mind under the shadow of burning coal
Don't worry my love
I am sleeping in your milky breast
And the game is played with the same rhythm
My hand on your tears
Sweetly is lost
Two thousand feet under the depth of time
My little bird

\*\*

The rivers of foolishness have come out of their usual stream,
The uncomforted lonelyness and the lonely star
Making their way with my passion.
In order to remember Spring,
Winter is coming rapidly and wearing its boring clothes,

You become upset with these quotes,
but Neruda said that love for his wife has two lives...
This is why he loved her even when he did not love her.

The hour of his poetry has been hit,
Surprisingly sadness and aesthetics of the bodlerian art
Are descending with nuances of anxiety over my pen
I have to indulge over mysterious labyrinths

The covers of this book are burned,
Love on poetry is never written.
Impossible to place an ocean of feelings in a book,
Impossible to place old feelings, there is room only for new ones

Herding my emotions,
Ready to jail them in verses
Worried to keep the metaphors
Nailed together with words.
It is hard to nail the feelings with big nails.
This is almost impossible.
In the father land of love my brush is sucking paint.
Just as in the erotic dream
I have to walk through Helena's bed,
To understand why she was the cause for the ancient tragedy,
And for the invention of Homer,
However have to learn how Serembe could walk through seas and oceans
With his small hands and being ill.

## Always Wanted To Let You Know

The sun can never be touched by hand,
Don't touch it, your fingers will melt
And your flesh will fall down
And consumed by fool cats.

Always wanted to let you know
And always to write,
To nail a verse
With great nostalgia
I have extremely wanted
In the mornings with Sun dew,
In the nights with Autumn storms,
Poetry cannot be killed,
Neither with weapons
Neither by Nuclear Weapons and foolish Kamikazes
More than every day, air and life
Always wanted to say, to never forget
Create your own kingdom of love night and day,
To fly to Copenhagen, to meet Hamlet
The dilemmas to be or not to be
Are not in the middle of the bluish sky and the black Earth
Skepticism is holding as a poisonous snake
Somewhere the sky explodes, in other place the word explodes,
Somewhere are living with words, Someone is killed for a word
Deep in the sky poetry is loudly crying
Every road has a meaning,
They have a name and a little history
Even though no one goes closer to Prometheus
Although shrank and narrowed,
Somewhere undeclared and declared,
Nontheless, it is possible to overcome obstacles,
With a few unsound letters to make poetry

Between the royal palaces and ancient crosses
Many paintings have their shades over our heads,
Those are shades beyond life and the muse of poetry
Smiles to Mona Lisa and says
Don't fall in love, be carefull it is just a net of provoking fairies
Even if you go to Paris,
To honor Victor Hygo's Cathedral,
In London is the endless magic mountain of honorable Shakespeare
Even if you go to Shkodër
To kiss the blooded feet of the lady of Shkodra,
To learn the mystery of the word, which is known only to her
Later to search for Father Fishta,
How he explodes with his metaphores in eternity
And to gather the bones through the torrential rivers.

## Question Mark

Distance is painted in a verse,
With broken color nuances
Amongst himself as in the mirror
Is broken the sky through dusk
Time is rinsing the brains
The word is burned on fire
Fire is lost in the word
Together with the words I am lost
Together with the verses I am burned
With the particles of the sky
That bite me
With their burned tears
Under the gurgling waters
I am watering the verses
Under the intoxicating whispers
With love
Nurturing rhymes, rhythms
Together, with the iron question marks
That are heavier today, tomorrow... for ever.
And today:
Broken verses
Twisted motives
Are attached axidentally to my verse
Not in the name of sanctity
Neither in the name of maliciousness
Full of misterious looks, faded and confused,
Are taged to my verse just as black spiders
Not only this
Love, They grabbed you fiercely
Songs of sluts expressing pain
For rotten times
And to the heavy heads
You trust everything
And don't understand the verse

Left in forgiveness
Cut in her throat
In magic places full of spiders,
In the extinguished tribes law towers
Oh Lord, My heart and love
Trust me
If life is fed with metaphors
And with rotten warms is fed
Or fed with art and love
Trust me
With killing metaphors
With poisonous screaming
With the hair which is not finding scissors
The walls of silence are unbreakable,
In the walls of obstacles
I pray to God,
Teach me not to love maliciousness as sanctity
Beyond thoughts are the heavy shadows of hopes.

## A Sea Of Nostalgia
*(To: Edita, my wife)*

From the Sun beans swallowed the fiery look
At this time when the World is suffering for a little love
As in sad dreams are suffering many spirits
Whose love is foreign
With anxiety and beattings
Today as a spring bird
You are breaking topics
Return topics

To love is the sanctified act of Earth
And the only virtue to live

A sea of nostalgia is filled with you

You hear how late light is screaming
And stars are kissing in their foreheads
Until we are kissed with the stars
We will wake up in the two poles,

How far away
Under the disturbed dreams our sleep in swimming
Night is wearing blackness, is thickened and is cold
And we feed ourselves with nostalgia
With ruined spirits we count our days with our fingers.

## As A Blue Bird Over Our Hands
*(To: My doughter, Isabela)*

Verses are scared from your soft look
Welcome, Isabella in the world of wonders

Your look is crossbreeding seasons
While overthrowing the rules

Over your eyes snow is melting in Sweden
January is not frozen anymore
Your mom covers you with feathers

My dear angel
Landed as a blue bird in our hands
As gifting the Sun to January

In the river of childhood dropped your look of an angel

A little salt to make life tastier
My dear Isabella, much better than paradise
Loved more than love itself
Shake the silent tales

The platoon of angels is screaming over our roads
You will never stop playing
We are returning from Desert
There is no Herodotus on Earth

## In the Life's Sky of Magic
*(To: My Son, Louis)*

Your name is being suspended and is the replica of the greatness of Jose Luis Borges,
He did not trust blindness, neither the preachers of darkness.
For the book's happiness
And for the seven nights of creation Homer was blinded
And you should extend your smile on Earth today,
The World desperately needs more happiness and less tragedy.

In the Winter forest of affliction the ice time is strangled.
April is the month of triumph, the month of flowers and births.
To be born means to enter in the big forest, Luis
Of endless dilemmas, in the forest with unresolved misteries.
The writters understood the ups and downs with the bible of silence
Which was singing on the mountains of Rugova.

Flowers are grown in April
April is the month of flowers, my dear son, Luis,
Is the month of births and singing birds

Abel's tower opens its arms,
Opens its doors for the scent of your breath,
They enter fearless

Times are kissed in their foreheads in the blue mornings with Sunshine
They work as usual,
Under the rainy nights with storms,
Don't ruin your deep sleep,
There are beatiful dreams, just as the whole life.
Don't ruin neither your sweet smile

## NDUE UKAJ - ITHACA OF THE WORD

Even if you see how the toungs are burned in the tower of Babel.
Never trust fake temples,
Times go and dissolve, while love remains the same.
Never trust darkness Luis
And write the Bible of life with nailed letters
You have many roads to walk and write.
Mother Theresa said that Love saves humanity
And you have your part in the Ocean of Salvage
Right your Bible every day and night
This way will overthrow darkness and muddy roads
Never relinquish research, -until infinity.
Don't forget in April are blossoming the smiles of winter.
Nature opens her eyes.
The song of Spring has sweet sounds, Beatiful birds singing.
And their song brings happyness to the high levels.
Just as the sweet morning smile
And your eye that encountered mom and dad
You are born to be loved and to love
In a beautiful day of Aesthetic symetry,
In a holy day with many verses.
In ten April sings the sky, and Earth is smiling.
Is the great week of the death of evil
And to the birth of life and love.
I have many things to say and write,
For the book of life and for our visits in church,
For the sounds of bells, and the calls of blessing
For the magic of love and the dreams of untouched height,
For the first tales, and imagination of the games
For the first ups and downs and endless adventures since the beggining
You are sunk in the magic depths in the most beautiful way possible.
We know that kingdom of the sky belongs only to kids,
The powerful empire in the eternal love.
Don't forget: In Spring always the flowers are blossoming,

Flowers are like the songs of soul
How beautiful it is to confess by yourself in the most beautiful way,
Without the need of metaphors, elegance and different poetic styles.
You are more than metaphors and styles,
In life there are many children born while dreaming love,
Strangle egoism, don't forget.
The world needs your smile.
In the depth of your marvellous imagination Times are met,
And you live to love and be loved.
I have a lot to write.
The bridges full of mysterious stories.
Somewhere over two thousand years, the World grows in the manger
And we walk through the endless dream.
Let the river of life flow freely on a forehead over time.
Never allow fool kings to bow on you
You are an angel born to love and be loved.
This is why you should walk assured in the life's magic sky...

## Life

When I say life is beautiful,

Through my ideas enters poetry
Beautiful as ever before with overwhelming reason
Dressed with a drape of shadow from her freightening eyes,
Thickened lips and a lustful red lipstick
In the bed of distracted Eros
Metaphors are proud that Life is beautiful
Even when there is pain
When grief encircles it
When the sky is melting on oil
And you are fed with tears and nostalgia,
Morning and night

Life is beautiful
Even when spirit is full of love,
Flies in the seventh sky
Life is beautiful,
Even when earthquakes ruin your soul
When love is dissolved in the nameless streets
And the rainbow is extinguished in your hands,
When you are exploding and exploding

Life is beautiful
An art mosaic of happiness
A spacious rainbow painted with many colors
Every day and night the wine glass is touching the sky
With the swallow I travel
In the torrential river
In forests of life searching for the tree of happiness

Life is beautiful
I don't want sadness
Neither when the sky is dark and your babies water their

chins
I love nature
Millions of attractions
I love the sky fully covered with fantasy.

Life is beautiful
When there is harmony
It has tears and pain
Never express yourself on canvas,
Don't stop happiness
With happiness live life

## From The Peakes Scratching The Sky Of Stubëll

Where hearts were cemented and Earth touches the sky in Stubëll,
Were the word was nailed, to preserve the speech
Mountains are resounding, they are rumbling,
The creeks of the village flowing tumultuously towards the nameless lakes

The peak of Stubëll standing over head
Magically kisses every morning with the sky

In Salonica left a piece of history,
The other remained somewhere in the roads of Asia, were turkish barbarians are rumbling
Another piece of Stubëll can be found in the mirror of Shkodra
My dear city of Stubëll, you never saw the Sun without the overwhelming mountain peak
And to learn the endless secrets without kissing your cross,

When your secrets are learned,
The ancient forgotten song will be performed...
The crumbled rocks have a fresh blood
Energetic romances kissed you, through the bloody fridays
The energy of bloody legs always went after you
You were engulfed very early with tears
And from tears exalted creeks arise
The truth is only known
Through the abrupt rocks and the beautiful hills
They know the unwritten depth of mortallity Fridays

## Ignored Longing

To walk on gorges the black river catches us
Our elastic penis has no energy
Is immune to dirtyness

Our wives keep it clean
Don't sleep with us

The battalions with artists build a chinese wall
Are confused from their views in Paris and London
And are sleeping drunk on the black sleep
Very sad

There is no such difficult thing as writing the art of ignorance
And the curse of oneself
In the shapes of a spider that strangles your breath

Fredrick Reshpi, with anxiety is detesting, these stupid ignorants

## We Grew With Tears

In my fifteenth birthday
Grandma told me:
 "The bloody moon
"Is looming over our heads..."
Later flattered my sweaty forehead,
With saddness sang for me:
We grew up with tears
While growing with the hunger
For words bread and time
For love peace and freedom
In the fields we had to water
The grain with tears

And the words continue to be wet with tears.

## Seasons Of My Life

Autumn
As always,
Is undressed quietly
Without the interiors,
The same as an old woman with wrinkles in her body,
Shy from her vanished beauty
Is laying down in front of the great Winter
To sleep under the fever of blunder
Winds
The storm
Everything is mad
Everywhere the signs of a ferocious winter
And a colorless Autumn

## Winter

The quilt of time's lust
The heavy snow and ice over our heads
As big as the idea of the fabulous winter
The frozen ice in the horizon of welcome
Is bloodening the spirit
There is no Sun
Coldness up to the bones
The soft bulbs are overwhelming
The bones are shaking in bed
With a deafening silence
There is no love
Saddness:
In the west there is no symptoms
Metamorphosis is jailed
The word Winter is strangling irony
And the myth of Spring
Spring
And...
Very happy
With delay
Remained without blossoming

## Epilogue

Never place a point to Poetry,
Never think in a epilogue
People always say:
The end cannot be found
Perfection is an Illusion
Epilogue is only the begining
Or the opposite
The end of the begining
2.
It is said the end cannot be found
Neither for poetry
Neither for love
I have to die
While singing for you
For your clean tears
For the lips blossoming in grave
For many many things...
And epilogue closes those in the begining
And the point is left in the pencil's edge.
3.
It is said that everything has an end
And in that end there is a begining
Including poetry
And love
Even for God that is crying
Even for the tear droping
And the graves of time is healing
This is the end of the begining
For the assasinated time,
With poisonous arrows in the forehead
For the frozen conscience
For the nasty verses
This is the end of a begining
For the fattened memory

For ignored dignity
In the cruel river
The canonical laws are reborn
The past is like a dream
This is the end of the begining
Which was lost just as the morning fog under the Sun
An epilogue killed in the morning

## For The Dissolved Time

SItuated in the middle of time
In the water shores without river
With the solitude grabbed as a bullet
With my strong hands,
Without my force when I was there
Opened my body
To feed
To thicken the time
To double its life
Saw the irregular face
Eyes in my forehead
Opened violently the time right up front
The eras thrown over the river
Saw my changed blood
Remained without a mouth, it was not me any more

## Poetry

When your spirit is filled with poison
When your brain is ignored
And the feelings are bitten,
When they steal your dreams
When your thoughts are killed in your forehead
When you don't have any one to speak with
To share a glass of Johny Walker
In the World walking with the wind
To squeeze the bolls full of sperm
Poetry is therapy
Don't scream
Don't cry
Don't write elegy and sad ballads
Keep away the sad verses full of tears
Don't decline your ambitions,
Look the poetry in her eyes
Feed yourself when bread is missing
Salt, is love and writing
Don't cry for solitude, never
Even when people ignore you
Nail and crucify you in the cross
Declaring as crazy
Attack your love
Poetry is salvation
A sweet scream with passion

## Walking with Verses

Over my head the sky was becoming dark
As the monster of the black night,
Over my head the sky was becoming dark
As the Earth was slippery below my feet
A drop of blood was multiplied just like the wind
Together with the sky was walking over my soil
With my verses as heavy as bullets
In the marathon of ideas without purpose
I am walking...
Over the Earth
Walking without a limit
Towards the time always walking
Until I strangle the antithesis
For you
And to transform the Globe
Into Happiness and joy

## The Castle of Love

The sounds of the broken guitar are singing
For your natural hair spreading over your soft shoulders
Amongst their aroma I am lost like a bird
Through the seven magic skies I fly
Under the autumn aroma my body is drunk,
Shaking and trembling just like the birds without a nest
The morning melodies are swallowed and attacked by obscured night
Solitude strangles in blood the sounds of the guitar
And from your eyes gathers the Sun shine
You are waiting near Hamlet's castle, and I am trembling under the castle of Ulpiana,
Until we depart to Prishtina, indeed this is just a short step for us.

You know this,
My sweet heart, Edita

## The Challenge

Fight with life if you can
Fight if you can by biting throats
Were the legends of ancient centuries kill
If you can fight with the times
Abandoned through the bloody rivers
If you can challenge mortality
You will remain an historic legend
If you can fight fanatism
With antichrist over the centuries
Recrucify it on the cross
Do everything if you can
Everything is possible
Plant all the flowers in a garden
They will remain without an aroma
If you can do anything,
Turn the devil into an angel
And dance with the ignorant
Very sad

## The Struggle

I have never believed that behind the rotten time
Memory is lost and imagination is overthrown
And in the human head are blossoming the warms
Together with the smelly snakes

Devils and angels
Eating and drinking
Speaking and lying
Smelling my cranium
With the lust of damn humans

An unseen dream
flowers droping blood
Dreams are bitten
Bitten aggressively
The rotter hairs are fighting
and their aroma is making us drunk

The pants that cannot hold our bolls
And sold in our markets
This is not a show of ideas

And the masks of the lying stages
And the gun fire like the fire with black smoke
My God, The same is happening as the mushroom after the rain is over
And, for the choir of ideas,
Scream ... where is the art?

## A MODERN LITERARY THEOLOGIAN

*(Excerpt from Afterword)*

Until today Ndue Ukaj has been a distinguished scholar in the fields of Comparative Litterature and as a freelance writer.

From now on Ukaj will establish himself as a poet. Indeed, his verses (are) and have been present in the daily and electronic press, but the book publication has a broader dimension and is received differently.

The author of this book does not belong to those writters surrounded by walls who explore the truth from within. Ukaj's verses represent a creative and vivid form of communication; with the dearest people in his heart, great public figures, with cultural and political contexts as well as empirical world, and of course, the history of literature...

Ndue Ukaj is not one of those writers who carve the word while reducing it down to its core, however he is an authority in the art of writing. The author's creativity is impulsive, touching and demanding; it is truly characterized by a cultural encyclopedia. In order to communicate with Ukaj's verses, the reader should be equiped with knowledge on mythological and biblical literature then historical and literary background; all these topics are intertwined in all poems of this volume. In Ukaj's verses are also short quotes from legendary figures such as Azem Shkreli or Mother Teresa which help the author to develop his lyrics.

The author has used the standard Albanian language, but for particular reasons, has used slang words in many poems.

## NDUE UKAJ - ITHACA OF THE WORD

Every poem represents a reader, and in the verses of Ukaj in some cases is spoken in the second person and in the others is used the third person. Ndue Ukaj has dedicated a large number of verses to his beloved wife (in the second person) and indeed these are the most achieved verses in the "Ithaca of the Word."

Ukaj has dedicated some poems to prominent figures in Local Culture, Humanism and Politics (Anton Pashku, Pjeter Bogdani, At Gjergj Fishta, Rifat Kukaj, Ibrahim Rugova, Mother Tereza, mainly developed in the third person but in the second person as well). These poems have minor sympathy complexion, but through it the author unravels sorrow and ideas. Ndue Ukaj reveals critical thoughts towards particular topics and exhilarates the visions for the future...

Ndue Ukaj has reserved the alchemist's mission for poetry and poets; this is the reason why he writes extensively. With the heart's calculus resolves the previously confusing and unknown facts. (Lonely poets)

Therefore, Ndue Ukaj highly believes that poets can change the world.

It is even mentioned in sacred texts that: the force of change can relocate mountains.

This is why I wish to emphasize again that:

*"Ndue Ukaj is a modern writer of psalms!"*

ANTON GOJÇAJ

## ABOUT THE AUTHOR:

Ndue Ukaj (1977) was born in the village of Upper Stubell, the district of Viti. Has received the degree of Bachelor of Arts from the University of Prishtina, Kosova, Department of Leters and Philosophy.

Mr. Ukaj has pursued Extensive Graduate Studies in Literature at the same Institution. Is the former Editor of the "Identiteti' magazine of Art, Culture and Society (2000-2001), published in Prishtina, Kosova. Is a regular contributor of the daily press in Albania and Kosova. Has authored many books on litterature and chritical essays, recently published in Albania, Kosova, Macedonia, Montenegro and in the diaspora. Many of his writing have been commented and translated in the distinguished international media.

During the Serbian occupation of Kosova, Ndue Ukaj has had a significant contribution in the political environment of Prishtina. During the recent years has been living and studying in Sweden. Is the Editor, has reviewed and written many introductions for over a dozen of projects. In 2004 published his book in Albanian, entitled: "Biblical Discourse in the Albanian Literature"; his works are also included in some anthologies and books of Albanian Poetry. Ndue Ukaj is one of the seven Albanian poets included in the Albanian – Romanian Anthology including seven Albanian and Romanian writters respectively ("Frumusetea frumusetilor," Bucharest , 2008).

Ndue Ukaj writes poetry, Essays, Prose, is a literary critic and writes articles in European daily press. Has a few writing projects in progress.

## TABLE OF CONTENT

Preface by Peter Tase.................................................5
Introduction by Petrit Palushi:
"Distinguished Aspects in Subject and Style"...............7
Godo is not coming. ...............................................11
The Emigrant..........................................................13
Hemingwayan waves of time.....................................15
Fatal Horse.............................................................17
Melancholy.............................................................19
Ruins of Love..........................................................20
Illusion of Time.......................................................22
The Waist of ime.....................................................23
Clashes..................................................................24
Small Steps.............................................................25
The Shadow of Crows...............................................26
The Painting of Love................................................27
The Trial of My Poetry.............................................28
My Alphabet...........................................................39
Illusion of a word....................................................30
Ancient Story..........................................................31
The Multi-Colored Time...........................................32
The Creation...........................................................34
As Usuall................................................................35
Drama...................................................................36
Compromise............................................................37
Marbled Memories...................................................38
Appeal...................................................................40
Lonely Poets...........................................................41
In a Technical Time..................................................42
The Autumn of Soul.................................................43
Voyage of the verse..................................................44
The Song of Light....................................................45
Only Silence...........................................................53
Memories are Broken in the Mirror............................59
Nostalgia................................................................61
Becoming a Poet......................................................62
The Candle.............................................................64
In Hamlet's Castle....................................................65
Six Letters..............................................................66
Black Time.............................................................67

# NDUE UKAJ - ITHACA OF THE WORD

To Father Peter Bogdani.................................................78
To Father Gjergj Fishta..................................................69
Mother Teresa................................................................70
Anton Pashku................................................................71
Ancient Dardania...........................................................72
The Poet (To Rifat Kukaj).............................................75
The Mother's Voice.......................................................77
The Kiss of the Star.......................................................78
Thirst..............................................................................79
Sickened Memory......................................................... 80
Taboo.............................................................................81
Philosophy of Foolishness.............................................82
Welcome........................................................................83
A Tragicomic Scene......................................................84
The Kiss.........................................................................85
The Aesthetics of Love.................................................86
Dilemma........................................................................88
A Song for the Song of Love........................................89
Dialogue........................................................................90
Today ............................................................................ 91
Save the Tears...............................................................93
Failing...........................................................................94
Succumbing..................................................................95
Autumn Night ..............................................................97
Your Fate...................................................................... 98
A Wound...................................................................... 100
The Meaning................................................................101
In Search of Lost Vocals.............................................102
Love in Darkness........................................................103
New Purpose...............................................................104
The Roots of the Tree.................................................105
Apocalypse..................................................................106
Tragic Aesthetics.........................................................107
Eclipse of Life.............................................................108
Perfected Time For Genocide.....................................109
Arguments of Time..................................................... 110
Fatherland....................................................................111
Love.............................................................................112
The Kingdom of Straws..............................................113
Kosova.........................................................................114
An Evening in Dubrovnik...........................................115
The Soul's Migration..................................................116
The Metaphor of Legend............................................ 117
Temptation..................................................................119

| | |
|---|---|
| We are All Odyssey | 121 |
| The Art of Love | 123 |
| Always wanted to let you know | 125 |
| Question mark | 127 |
| A Sea of Nostalgia | 139 |
| As a Blue Bird over our Hands | 130 |
| In the Life's Sky of Magic | 131 |
| Life | 134 |
| From the peakes scratching the sky of Stubëll | 136 |
| Ignored Longing | 137 |
| We Grew with Tears | 138 |
| Seasons of my Life | 139 |
| Winter | 140 |
| Epilogue | 141 |
| For The Dissolved Time | 143 |
| Poetry | 144 |
| Walking with verses | 145 |
| The Castle of Love | 146 |
| The Challenge | 147 |
| The Struggle | 148 |
| A Modern Literary Theologian By Anton Ggojçaj | 149 |
| About the Author | 151 |
| Table of Content | 153 |